THE
SOFT COATED
WHEATEN TERRIER

Coat of Honey~Heart of Gold

ROBERTA A. VESLEY

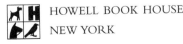
HOWELL BOOK HOUSE
NEW YORK

To Debbie, Nancy, Emily, and Henry

Howell Book House
Hungry Minds, Inc.
909 Third Avenue
New York, NY 10022
www.hungryminds.com

For general information on Hungry Minds' products and services please contact our Customer Care Department; within the U.S. at 800-762-2974, outside the U.S. at 317-572-3993 or fax 317-572-4002.

Library of Congress Cataloging-in-Publication Data
Vesley, Roberta.
The soft coated wheaton terrier: coat of honey, heart of gold/Roberta A. Vesley
      p.cm.
    Includes bibliographical references (pp. 170-173) and index.
    ISBN 1-58245-017-X
    1. Soft coated wheaton terrier.   I. Title.
    SF429.S69V475 1998
    636.755—dc21   98-42648
                            CIP

Manufactured in the United States of America

14 13 12 11 10 9 8 7 6 5 4 3 2

Cover and book design by George J. McKeon

Acknowledgments

I was raised to say "please" and "thank you" at the appropriate times. While writing this new book, I used the first word often to secure photographs, statistics and other information I needed to make the project truly complete. Now it is time for me to say "thank you" to all those generous Wheaten fanciers who willingly came through. I was gratified at the response to my requests for photos on the Wheaten "L."

While I cannot thank all my contributors and helpers individually, there are a few who went beyond the call of duty and friendship. I am especially grateful to Gay Dunlap for writing the Foreword. Again, Marjorie Shoemaker graciously allowed me to use her show grooming instructions and drawings. Thanks to Sally Sotirovich for allowing me to wade through her photograph collection. Thanks also to her sister, Barbara Kolk, AKC Librarian, for sending information promptly and efficiently.

I will be eternally grateful that the Soft Coated Wheaten Terrier Club of America is so deeply dedicated to documenting breed history that it publishes the *Yearbook*. I treasure the two hardcover volumes in my personal library and recommend them to every Wheaten owner who wants to know from where the Soft Coated Wheaten Terrier came.

As usual, my ever patient husband, Allan, did yeoman's work, both in inspiring my creative muse and in doing the drudge work needed to produce a manuscript. I thank him sincerely. Thanks also to my son-in-law,

Joseph Hargitai, for getting my old manuscript disk into a readable format and for taking the photograph of Kate and me.

Most of all, my sincere thanks to my editor, Seymour Weiss, for his patience and understanding. They say timing is everything in life. This was not the ideal time in my life to be writing a book, but Seymour's caring advice and support pulled me through. I appreciate his efforts and consideration more than I can say.

Contents

(Diane Fleming)

Foreword

There was a time when no one had any interest in publishing a book about the Soft Coated Wheaten Terrier. Reasons related, understandably from a publisher's perspective, to the ubiquitous concerns over sales potential. The contention of various publishing houses was that there simply was not sufficient interest in the breed. Therefore, to publish a book about this Johnny-come-lately to the Terrier Group appeared totally unwarranted and financially unfeasible. They were, of course, wholly oblivious to the purchasing power of Wheaten owners who, in frenzied fashion, were buying up everything related to the breed. Terrier artifacts, if even only vaguely suggestive of a Wheaten, were quickly scooped up by breed devotees. It was the early 1970s and we were hungering for a book about the Soft Coated Wheaten Terrier.

The only reference work in print at that time was *How to Raise and Train a Soft-Coated Wheaten Terrier*. Margaret O'Connor who, along with her family, had accelerated interest in the breed in North America during the late 1950s and the 1960s wrote the breed-specific portion of this sixty-four-page paperback. We treasured that book for the marvelous photos of our dogs' progenitors, but we mostly treasured it because it was all we had. We wanted more.

In 1977 Maureen Holmes, Ireland's matriarch of the breed, saw to it that her first book, *The Wheaten Years*, was privately published in the United States. With page upon page of unidentified dogs, sketchy information about North American involvement in the breed and no reference to the Soft Coated Wheaten Terrier abroad, it was a disappointment to many. We still needed a truly definitive book that told it all.

Then, as luck would have it, Roberta Vesley entered the employ of the American Kennel Club. "Pan," as she is fondly known to her friends and family, had purchased her first Wheaten, Lady Patricia of Windmill, in 1969. In those days, club membership was granted to anyone registering a dog with the fledgling Soft Coated Wheaten Terrier Club of America and, as a result, most of us found ourselves totally immersed in breed activities. Pan was no exception, showing "Kelly" in fun matches, whelping several litters and serving on SCWTCA's Board of Directors. These activities cemented her connection to both the breed and other Wheaten devotees. Although her new job at the AKC precluded active participation of this sort, Pan retained close ties to the breed she loves.

In 1979, Pan was appointed director of the AKC's impressive, extensive library. As a result, she found herself armed with first-hand knowledge regarding the dearth of reliable information about the Soft Coated Wheaten Terrier. She joked that it seemed as though there were 25,000 volumes about dogs in general, many on terriers in particular, but that the search for data about the Wheaten was not unlike an archeological dig. Running into stone walls was not unusual. When data was retrieved it was exasperatingly fragmented.

Pan's deep connection to the breed succored a strong desire to compile the available fragmented data. This aspiration led to an intensive search for every scrap of information she could uncover and led to interviews with the early pioneers, most of whom were still around at that time. Then, with the help of Seymour Weiss, an editor with Howell Book House and a terrier fancier himself, Pan convinced Elsworth Howell that a comprehensive book about the breed was not only needed, but also in great demand. Wheaten owners across the land were eagerly opening their pocketbooks, and she was certain they would buy her book. *The Complete Soft Coated Wheaten Terrier* was published in 1991, and she was right. We are now looking at a new book based on this valuable, landmark resource work.

In her first book, Pan wrote of following an untried path and the difference it made in her life. "This book," she noted, "is my way of sharing the story of that journey with all those whose enchantment is yet to come."

Pan's knowledge and love for the breed emanate from each page. Those of us who have shared her passion all these years as well as those yet to experience the enchantment fundamental to owning a Soft Coated Wheaten Terrier will be drawn to this new addition to the literature of the breed.

GAY DUNLAP
Gleanngay
Santa Fe, New Mexico
July, 1998

Introduction

When I wrote my earlier book, *The Complete Soft Coated Wheaten Terrier,* I was candid in saying that it was a very personal account and was influenced by my own experiences with the animals and by my relationships with many Wheaten fanciers that I knew so well.

Much has changed since then. For one thing, Wheatens have become much more popular and can no longer be thought of as a rare breed. Secondly, my own direct involvement with the breed has lessened. There are many more people breeding and showing these dogs, and I can no longer claim to know all of them. In addition, since I have retired from my career with the American Kennel Club, I am no longer in professional contact with many of the intricacies of the dog world. Finally, while I am still a devoted member of The Soft Coated Wheaten Terrier Club of America, I no longer serve on its Board of Directors or as its Public Information Chairman.

The net result of these changes is that I have been able to step back and take a more detached, objective look at the subject. I am still just as enamored of and fascinated by this, my absolute favorite dog breed. Wheatens mean more to me now than they ever have. Now I am able to place myself in the position of the many people who have seen and admired Soft Coated Wheaten Terriers, but who are not fully familiar with them. If my first book was mainly addressed to the insiders in the breed, this one is addressed to the wider audience that has not yet, or is only beginning to share, the great enjoyment and satisfaction that Wheaten ownership can bring.

In this book I have introduced many of the newer breeders and exhibitors who will have the responsibility for continuing the progress that the breed has made over the last several decades. They give us great cause to be optimistic and enthusiastic about the future. I have tried to describe the connection that their dogs have to the breed's illustrious past.

On the other hand, I have also described some of the health problems that have become of considerable concern to all Wheaten enthusiasts. But even here, there is reason to be hopeful. The support that Wheaten people are providing to veterinary researchers is extraordinary. We can only sincerely hope that their efforts will enable us to predict, diagnose and treat some of the ailments occurring in this overwhelmingly healthy, robust breed.

The sections on training, grooming and diet are more detailed than those provided in the earlier book. I have also included more information on routine maintenance and health care. It is my hope that this will help new owners to enjoy their Wheatens more fully and more responsibly than would otherwise be possible.

The American Kennel Club has instituted new performance activities such as Agility and the Canine Good Citizen program that provide opportunities for Wheaten owners to interact with their dogs in a positive, rewarding fashion. I have attempted to whet owners' appetites for participating in these exciting and worthwhile ventures.

My involvement with Soft Coated Wheaten Terriers over the past thirty years has added a wonderful dimension to my life. The Wheaten may not be the right breed for everyone but it suits me perfectly. I hope that this book expresses my love and enthusiasm for the breed and that it will help many others to share that experience.

(photo by Jane Elkin Thomas)

CHAPTER 1

Profile of the Soft Coated Wheaten Terrier—Is It Right for You?

What's in a name? In the case of the Soft Coated Wheaten Terrier, quite a lot. Many breed names tell us something of the breed's place of origin or the tasks for which the breed was developed. Few names, however, are as truly descriptive as is the Wheaten's. It is a name that calls to mind the soft, flowing coat and the rich golden wheat color that is the breed's most distinguishing feature. But in addition, the name tells us that the dog is part of the Terrier Group, with all of the behavioral and personality traits that characterize those particular breeds.

But a name is still very much a short-hand symbol for the much larger constellation of physical appearance and behavioral patterns that make a specific breed of dog a unique occupant of the animal kingdom. To fill out the description we need a word picture of a breed, which takes the form of a breed Standard.

According to the Standard for the Soft Coated Wheaten Terrier, the dog is described as "a medium sized, hardy, well balanced sporting terrier, square in outline . . . distinguished by his soft, silky, gently waving coat of warm wheaten color . . . steady disposition . . . moderation both in structure and presentation . . . alert and happy animal, graceful, strong and well coordinated." (The Standard is discussed in depth in Chapter 3.) This Standard tells us what a Wheaten looks like, but beyond "alert and happy," there is little to describe the "character" of the breed. Regarding this very important side to the breed, we need to know more.

During the years I served as information director for the Soft Coated Wheaten Terrier Club of Metropolitan New York, much of our early promotional literature described the Wheaten as "a medium sized, blonde shaggy dog that does not shed." There is something about a hairy dog that appeals to people. Many Wheaten owners will openly admit that the "shaggy look" was what first attracted them to the breed. Then, as now, the question I was most frequently asked by prospective owners and novices is "does the dog shed?" The answer is a qualified "no." Wheatens shed, but minimally. Because of their single coat, when hairs do break off, they usually get caught in the coat and eventually cause mats. This trait makes the Wheaten a "high maintenance" breed requiring regular, thorough combing and brushing. It is widely believed that a dog with a low-shedding factor is a better companion for people with allergies, but the lack of shedding is not a guarantee that these people will be totally symptom-free. Some people with allergies to dogs are not sensitive to the hair but to the naturally occurring dander all dogs carry. If a potential buyer has allergies to animals, it would be wise for him or her to visit a home with at least one Wheaten in residence to see whether any adverse reactions occur.

But what is a Soft Coated Wheaten Terrier besides a "medium-sized, blonde, shaggy dog that doesn't shed?" First of all, the Wheaten is a dog. This means that like any dog, he has hair, he barks as the spirit moves him, he jumps on people and chases cats, squirrels, balls, sticks and Frisbees. Being a dog also means that the Soft Coated Wheaten Terrier is a pack animal and looks to you as his leader. If you do not establish yourself as the "alpha" or head dog, you are unlikely to have a satisfactory relationship with a Wheaten. Wheatens will press to make themselves the dominant pack member, but they will readily accept you as the leader if you are firm, consistent and fair.

TERRIER HERITAGE

A Wheaten is also a terrier. This adds another dimension to his character. Many people are put off by the reputation terriers have for being noisy, aggressive and hyperactive. It does take a special type of person to own terriers. One has to accept them as they are: lively, curious and affectionate. They are strong-willed and this sometimes leads people to describe them as stubborn. A quick look at their heritage helps explain this behavior.

The word "terrier" is from the Latin word "terra," meaning earth. These dogs were bred to go "to ground," that is, they would enter the lair of a fox, badger or rat to kill or force their prey into the open. Unlike the gundogs of the nobility, their lives were hard, and they had to work for whatever meager rewards they got. However, terriers also lived in close proximity to their owners, and thus their affectionate nature developed with great intensity. Many a Wheaten owner can vouch for the fact that Wheatens, unlike most of the larger terriers, go "to ground"—and the holes in their back yards and gardens are ample proof. Given the opportunity, most Wheatens will catch mice and rats. I recently heard of one Wheaten who fought and killed full-grown raccoons on two separate occasions. Brave dog!

Gameness is another trait for which terriers were specifically developed. The word means that the dog has "fighting spirit or pluck." Anyone who has watched some of the other terrier breeds at a show, has seen them "face off" and sometimes exhibit a great deal of gameness, originally intended for use on vermin.

The Wheaten is normally much less aggressive than other terriers. This is due to his historic use as a worker on Irish farms. Wheatens rarely start fights, but will not back down when challenged. When the breed was first recognized by the American Kennel Club, there was a faction in the fancy that wanted the Wheaten placed in the Working Group, but the majority voted for inclusion in the Terrier Group which is as it should be, and where the breed has prospered.

Wheatens are typically high-energy dogs, as this four-month-old clearly demonstrates. (photo by Susan Saltzman)

GENERAL CHARACTER

So here we have a medium-sized, blonde, shaggy dog who sheds little, goes to ground and exhibits fighting spirit and pluck when it is appropriate to do so. But the Wheaten is more than this. The breed is lively, affectionate, curious and alert to anything out of the ordinary. He cannot truly be called a guard dog, but he is definitely protective of his family and his territory. Wheatens have alerted their families to danger on more than one occasion.

When a visitor is admitted to the home, a Wheaten will accept the stranger's greeting and will most likely jump straight off the floor to offer a wet, welcoming kiss. As a result, a Wheaten owner may lose some non-doggy friends. The

Wheaten's herding heritage will often be observed when a dog "circles" a guest. Once a Wheaten knows you, you have a friend for life. Wheatens have long memories of friend and foe alike. While moderation is a key word in describing the Soft Coated Wheaten Terrier, the breed is far from moderate in its loyalty and affection.

Wheatens are definitely "people" dogs. They want to be where their family is. They do not take as kindly to kennel situations as do some other breeds. Wheatens are not "yappy," but they will bark when there is a reason. Some tend to "talk" (with an amazing repertoire of vocalizations) to their owners when they want something.

Wheatens are easy keepers. They do not require fancy furnishings. Most seek the coolness of a hard floor for sleeping. I've owned Wheatens who constantly removed bedding from their crates, preferring to lie on the bare surface. However, older dogs often welcome a soft, warm surface on which to sleep. Be advised, if you encourage your dog to join you on the furniture, he surely will take advantage of the opportunity to come up on a regular basis.

Wheatens, true to their terrier heritage, will chase brooms, mops, vacuum cleaners and feather dusters. This makes housecleaning a bit of a challenge. My best advice is to clean when the dog is in his crate or run, and so not available to help you. You may find that your Wheaten has a penchant for used tissues and the baby's diapers. It is important to discard such items so that the dog cannot reach them. If you provide the proper toys for your puppy, you should not have problems with him chewing anything undesirable.

Wheatens like to be in charge of whatever is going on around them. "Fraser" (Bumblebeary's First Admiral) takes the helm. (photo by Sandy Neufeld)

Wheatens adapt to nearly any environment. Just before I bought my first Wheaten, *New York* magazine carried an article that billed the Wheaten as "the perfect apartment dog." The Wheaten's medium size is certainly a distinct advantage for urban residents, but some breeders will not sell a dog to city apartment dwellers. However, the fact that most Wheatens are not yappy is another asset

Wheatens were bred to go "to ground." This scene is at an earth dog trial, but a Wheaten will not hesitate to dig his own holes in your backyard. (photo by Elena Landa)

that helps make the breed a good apartment dog. However, it should be remembered that the Wheaten is a high-energy breed and even in an urban situation, sufficient exercise is vital. A tired dog is a good dog.

TRAINABILITY AND PHYSICAL NEEDS

For the most part, Wheatens are easily trained. They do better with obedience training than most other terrier breeds. Many have been used as Therapy Dogs. With a Wheaten, as with most dogs, the important thing is to let him know what you want him to do. Training should be firm, fair and consistent from the time he becomes part of your family.

Experts agree that behavior problems are a major reason for dogs being given up to humane societies and shelters. The abundance of local legislative proposals to restrict dog ownership is symptomatic of anti-dog feeling in this country. Anyone who owns a Wheaten must make a commitment to become a responsible dog owner. This means teaching your dog basic obedience. A well-behaved dog is a pleasure and the time spent training is beneficial to the dog, the owner and the community.

It is vital that you establish your position as pack leader from day one. As stated above, Wheatens will jump straight up to give a greeting. This is, however, unacceptable behavior. The puppy must be trained not to jump. Remember that adorable puppy will weigh between thirty-five and forty-five pounds when grown and could injure a child or adult simply out of exuberance.

Most areas have an obedience club that offers fairly inexpensive training classes. AKC can provide you with a list of clubs in your area. In lieu of formal classes, videotapes and books are also readily available. A list is included in the bibliography at the end of this book. Spend some time studying even before you get your dog. The effort you expend learning about how dogs behave before your puppy comes into your home will help make you a more confident, responsible owner.

Wheatens have a strong herding instinct and when sheep are not available, people become the focus of this instinctive behavior. (photo by Judy Price)

The Wheaten is basically a healthy breed. Most hobby breeders and the Soft Coated Wheaten Terrier Club of America are truly concerned about the breed and its future. The SCWTCA requires its member/breeders to x-ray breeding stock for evidence of hip dysplasia and to have eyes checked for progressive retinal atrophy. Cases of these conditions are uncommon, but it is only through awareness that they can be controlled.

The Soft Coated Wheaten Terrier Club of America, in conjunction with the American Kennel Club's Canine Health Foundation, is sponsoring research into kidney disease that appears to be present in the breed. Results are not yet conclusive, however. (See Chapter 6.)

A moderate amount of exercise will keep your Wheaten fairly fit. However, he will absolutely thrive on regular, vigorous exercise. The breed is naturally sturdy and well muscled. A Wheaten owner has to be willing to take the time and energy to provide the exercise needed to maintain good muscle tone and condition. Needless to elaborate, the effort will also benefit the physical fitness of the owner.

WHEATENS AND CHILDREN

General books about choosing a dog breed usually spend a significant amount of space discussing the child/dog

A happy owner holding a seven-month-old Wheaten puppy. Sara Hill's Lady Be Good is quite a handful. (photo by Amy Havely)

relationship. Wheatens tend to be rated quite favorably in this regard. However, every dog is an individual—as is every child. I currently own a Wheaten who has never jumped on a child, but I have owned one whom I could not trust with children at all.

A Wheaten may be too exuberant for a toddler. If there are small children in your household and you've set your heart on a Wheaten, wait until your children are older and can appreciate and understand how to treat a dog properly. No matter how well behaved your Wheaten and your children are, adult supervision is a must when dogs and children are together. Remember, kids will be kids and dogs will be dogs.

Whether you choose a puppy or adult, you should recognize that the "coat," the hallmark of the breed that first attracted you to Wheatens, is also the breed's major disadvantage. A Wheaten coat is like Velcro. It attracts all sorts of leaves, twigs and grass. It takes regular care to keep the Wheaten coat clean, healthy and tangle free. A matted or shaved Wheaten is not a pretty sight. The coat protects the dog from weather and is not meant to be shaved down. Study Chapter 8,

Wheatens are sensitive to their owners' moods and willingly share quiet times as well as periods of hard-charging activity. (photo by Sydney Fisher)

"Grooming the Soft Coated Wheaten Terrier," to make sure you want to make the commitment to be owned by a Soft Coated Wheaten Terrier. Remember the dogs you see at the shows and in the beautiful photos in dog books don't just grow that way. So if you are not willing to make this commitment to the dog's appearance and good health, choose a breed with more modest grooming requirements.

(photo courtesy of Betsy Geertson)

CHAPTER 2

A Brief History of the Soft Coated Wheaten Terrier

THE DOG IN HISTORY

In order to better understand what a Soft Coated Wheaten Terrier is all about, it is important to know about its ancestors and how it developed into the dog we have today. It is also helpful to consider the history of Ireland, its country of origin, and what life there was like. The story presented here is based on the extensive research that I did for *The Complete Soft Coated Wheaten Terrier*.

In *The Lessons of History*, by Will and Ariel Durant, the authors state "Most history is guessing, and the rest is prejudice." These words are particularly appropriate in a study of almost any breed of dog. Some breeds, like the Saluki and the Mastiff, have well-documented histories that date back to antiquity. When it comes to terriers in general, and the Soft Coated Wheaten Terrier in particular, the matter is far from clear. Almost every writer who addresses the history of terriers describes their origins as "being lost in the mists of time" or "obscured by myth and legend" or similar words. They are quite right.

There is a wealth of material in the literature of the dog regarding hounds, other hunting dogs and royal lap dogs, but one must make a determined search for mention of the terriers, since theirs were usually humble origins; they did not have the more elevated status of other breeds.

In England, King Canute (d.1035) established the first Laws of the Forest, which probably also applied in Ireland. Under these laws, only freemen and landowners were permitted to have hunting dogs. The peasants were allowed to have small dogs who were incapable of killing large game.

References to terrier-like dogs appear as early as A.D. 221 in a work by Oppian. *The Boke of St. Albans* by Dame Juliana Berners (printed in 1486, but probably written earlier) mentions terriers among a list of British breeds. In Abraham Fleming's 1576 translation of Johannes Caius' *De Cannibus Britannicis* terriers are described thus:

> *a sorte there is which hunteth the Foxe and the Badger or Greye onely, whom we call Terrars, because they (after the manner and custom of Ferrets in searching for Connyes) creepe into the grounde, and by that meanes make afrayde, nyppe and byte the Foxe and the Badger . . . that eyther they teare them in peeces with thayre teeth . . . or else hayle and pull them perforce out of their . . . close caves, or . . . drive them out . . .*

Based on what the early works on dogs tell us, we can accept the fact that a small- to medium-sized, keen-scented dog existed on the European continent and in the British Isles for a long time, in spite of the lack of concrete evidence. The Celtic breeds were known throughout the ancient world. Life in ancient Ireland was harsh and cruel. The island was subjected to wave after wave of invasion. Typically, these invaders settled there and became more Irish than the Irish. Their dogs most likely accompanied them and, by the operation of natural selection, bred with the existing dogs.

Among these early dogs were the ancestors of the terriers. They were small, hardy animals who kept houses and barns free of vermin for rich and poor alike and supplied the farmer's family with a steady supply of small game. These dogs were also used for menial kitchen tasks such as turning the spit. They were tough little dogs and because of their harsh existence, only the strongest among them survived.

THE IRISH CONNECTION

In the British Isles, serious and conscientious dog breeding did not become widespread until the last half of the nineteenth century. The first organized

Woodcut from Thomas Bewick's A General History of Quadrapeds.

dog show was held in 1859 in Newcastle-on-Tyne. In England, the Kennel Club was established in 1873 to regulate shows and record pedigrees. (Until 1922, when the Irish Kennel Club was founded, the Kennel Club also regulated Irish dog activities.) In Ireland, where most large game had become extinct, large dogs were too expensive for most people to keep. As a result, many fanciers turned to the terriers as an outlet for their dog activities.

Ireland was a land of few cities and many small villages. In these isolated towns, local dogs would breed indiscriminately, and in time they would all come to resemble each other. Owners were reluctant to share these animals with outsiders, and thus the local types remained relatively pure because of the small gene pool. It is from these local types that the Irish Terrier, the Kerry Blue Terrier and the Soft Coated Wheaten Terrier all evolved.

The history of the Soft Coated Wheaten Terrier is closely related to that of the Irish Terrier and Kerry Blue Terrier. Many early fanciers believed that the Wheaten was the progenitor of the other two breeds even though the Irish Terrier and Kerry Blue Terrier were recognized as separate breeds earlier than the Soft Coated Wheaten Terrier.

In some of the early dog shows an "Irish" terrier was any terrier that was bred in Ireland. Thus, classes were made up of dogs of all types. In Vero Shaw's *Illustrated Book of the Dog* (1881) an 1876 show was described:

Illustration of an Irish Terrier from Vero Shaw's Illustrated Book of the Dog. *Note that the coat appears to be longer and more open than that of a modern Irish Terrier.*

. . . *The variety was more than charming, it was ridiculous; reports say there was no attempt at type in particular, no style; long legs, short legs, hard coats, soft coats, thick short skulls and long lean ones; all were there. 'Long, low and useful dogs' were held up for admiration. Long and useful, if you like, but never low for an Irish Terrier.*

The best known dog books of the 1800s described "Irish" terriers of all sizes, colors and coat types. Writers talk of origins "lost in antiquity" and descriptions in old Irish manuscripts (which, to my knowledge, have never been verified). Edward Ash, in his seminal book *Dogs: Their History and Development*, wrote:

Kathleen, the first Irish Terrier shown in America in 1880. (photo from James Watson's Dog Book, *1905)*

. . . no one appears to have provided nor given the statement on which the claim of antiquity is based.

Ash goes on to say:

. . . we find that 1872, 1873 and 1874 are the years when the Irish Terrier first of all claimed attention and even then what type an Irish Terrier should be was a matter of opinion.

By 1879 a club for the Irish Terrier had been formed and a standard of points was written that set the "type" for what is the present-day Irish Terrier. The rich red color and hard, dense coat, intelligence, fiery expression and size were selectively bred for. The Irish Terrier is a lighter, racier animal than its two cousins, the Wheaten and the Kerry Blue, but it evolved from the same stock.

THE KERRY BLUE CONNECTION

Let us look at one of the oldest myths about the Wheaten and the Kerry: the story of the blue dog who survived a shipwreck off the coast of Ireland after the defeat of the Spanish Armada. This famous traveler is purported to have swum ashore and bred with the native wheaten terriers to produce the Kerry. This makes for a wonderfully romantic story.

There are a number of things to ponder about this theory. First of all, would the Spanish have taken dogs with them in their quest to conquer England? They did take horses and mules to use in the hopes for battles on land. These were dumped into the sea after their defeat by the English.

If they did have dogs with them, what kind would they have been? Some of the ships in the Armada were probably Portuguese. Is it possible that the famous blue dog was a Portuguese Water Dog? Isn't it interesting to note that the Portie has a single, non-shedding coat that occurs in both a wavy variety and a curly one? Mrs. Maureen Holmes, author of *The Wheaten Years* staunchly maintains that the storied blue dog was a Russian dog from a Russian ship that broke up in a storm in 1758.

I cannot accept the Armada story. However, I can believe that Portuguese sailors had commerce with the Irish. Historically, the Portuguese were known for their ability as seamen. And they did take their dogs with them. They are known to have fished off the coast of Newfoundland in the 16th and 17th centuries. They also sailed to Iceland.

Ireland was a convenient place to stop for supplies and trade.

From what the early dog writers told us, the various terrier-like dogs in Ireland came in a variety of colors, sizes, shapes and coat types. By breeding for specific traits, breed type can be stabilized in relatively few generations, and this is probably what happened with the evolving terrier varieties of Ireland.

Perhaps there was a shipwrecked blue dog. It is equally possible that Portuguese Water Dogs were a factor. In any case it is interesting to note that black puppies occur in Wheaten litters, and Maureen Holmes showed me a fairly recent photo of a wheaten-colored Kerry Blue Terrier at our meeting in 1989. Let us now consider some of the known background of the Kerry Blue Terrier.

One of the earliest mentions of the Kerry Blue Terrier is in Herbert Compton's *Twentieth Century Dogs* (1904). The dog is described as a "silver-haired or slaty-blue terrier in County Limerick," in a section about terriers in Ireland.

Engraving showing various types of terriers from Stonehenge's Dogs of the British Islands.

In 1887, silver-haired terriers were shown again in Limerick. Five years later, Irish Terriers (Blue) were shown in Killarney, and in 1902 a class for Blue Terriers (Working) had fourteen entries.

In the late 1800s, through careful, selective breeding the slate blue color became firmly established but the breed itself was not recognized by the Kennel Club until 1920. World War I was probably a factor in the delay. Kerries became more popular in England because they were shown trimmed. In Ireland they are still shown untrimmed while the reverse is true for the Wheaten.

COUSINS UNDER THE SKIN

As we have looked at the histories of the Irish Terrier and the Kerry, we have found mention of what must have been the progenitors of the Soft Coated Wheaten Terrier. Long-legged terriers with soft, open coats of wheaten color are frequently described in reports of early shows. However, it was not until the 1930s that the Wheaten attracted

The Irish Blue Terrier as depicted in Pierce O'Connor's book, Sporting Terriers.

the interest of terrier fanciers. It is certain that wheaten-colored terriers with soft, open coats existed in Ireland in the 1800s. What is not certain is whether they existed as a separate breed as long ago as the other chroniclers of the breed aver.

In the search for a new "star" in the terrier world, the Wheaten was a logical candidate. Success would require defining, refining and promoting this sturdy, inherently beautiful and game animal. According to Maureen Holmes in *The Wheaten Years*, the Wheaten's rise to stardom began in 1932 when a Wheaten turned in an outstanding performance in a field trial for terriers. Several of the participants and spectators were so favorably impressed that they decided to form a club and work for recognition of the breed.

In the December 1933 issue of the *Irish Field*, the writer, Danny Boy, comments on the death of a Mr. Harry Dixon as ". . . a great fancier of the Wheaten Terrier, Harry maintained that for gameness and intelligence, the dog had no equal, his own terrier, Captain, being a fine example of this contention." (There is a dog called "Captain" that appears in old Irish pedigrees and just dead-ends. We don't know if this is the same dog, as "Captain" has always been a popular name for dogs.)

When I wrote *The Complete Soft Coated Wheaten Terrier* (New York: Howell Book House, 1992), I used the periodical *Irish Field* for much of the information. I never discovered the identity of the columnist, Danny Boy. However, I recently received a letter from Bruce Sussman, who was once active in Wheatens and who now owns a Glen of Imaal Terrier. In researching that breed, he came across a reference to Danny Boy in a monograph called *Ireland's Native Terrier, The Glen of Imaal Reference Book* produced and edited by Eithne Cleary (copyright worldwide):

> *Mr. Daniel O'Donoghue writing under the nom de plume Danny Boy gave a great boost to the breed, at this time he was representing the Dublin Irish Blue Terrier Club on an Ard Chomhairle. (page 7)*
> *The Breed Club was strong until 1939, when Mr. Daniel O'Donoghue retired as secretary . . . (page 8)*

Bruce also discovered a kennel in Ireland, active in the 1930s through the 1950s, using the name Hacketstown that produced both Glens and

Wheatens. A famous Glen was named Hacketstown Lad, a name which also appears in Wheaten pedigrees. Among Glen of Imaal Terrier fanciers it is rumored that a litter was born in which some dogs were registered as Glens and some as Wheatens.

Going back to *The Wheaten Years*, Maureen Holmes—who bred and showed Wheatens for over forty years—says a club was formed in 1932 to promote and seek recognition for the Wheaten Terrier. The *Irish Field* first mentions the Irish Wheaten Terrier Club in its April 1, 1936, issue. Acceptance of the Wheaten as a breed was strongly opposed by both the Irish Terrier Club and Glen of Imaal Club.

Mrs. Maureen Holmes, the moving force in the early years of the modern Wheaten in Ireland, is shown with Emily Holden and an Irish-bred dog.

RECOGNITION IN IRELAND

By 1937, Wheaten interest had expanded. The Wheaten Club was well organized and was supported by friends in high places in the "official" dog world. When the Club agreed to change the breed name to "Soft Coated Wheaten Terrier," acceptance was assured

A panel of experts was set up to determine whether individual dogs were indeed Soft Coated Wheatens. This procedure was eliminated once a number of Wheatens became champions. At last, the Wheaten had official recognition.

During the next ten years a total of ten Wheatens finished their championships. The breed became eligible for registration in England in 1943 even though championship status was not granted until much later. Activity in Ireland increased when Maureen Holmes became involved. From 1943, when she whelped her first Wheaten litter, until her death in 1996, Mrs. Holmes was a potent force in the breed.

When the breed was first accepted, it was necessary for a dog to win in field trials as well as on the show bench in order to become a champion. This requirement was eliminated by IKC in 1968. The early history of the Wheaten Terrier is inseparable from the history of dogs in general and terriers in particular. We have followed the stories of the Irish Terrier, the Kerry Blue and briefly mentioned the Glen of Imaal, then we came back to the Soft Coated Wheaten Terrier. We examined facts and looked at the legends. We have brought the Wheaten to the time of its first trip across the Atlantic. While the breed is old, it is probably not as ancient as we would like to believe. A quote from Anna Redlich's *Dogs of Ireland* puts the whole thing in perspective: "And, after all, are not the results of the evolution of a breed more important than its origin?"

ACROSS THE POND

Prior to the end of World War II there is almost no mention of the breed in the United States. There is the description in *The American Book of the Dog* (1889), of the wheaten-colored Irish Terriers with soft, open coats.

A "yellow North of Ireland Terrier" was shown at Westminster in October 1878, a show which predates the establishment of the AKC. These dogs could have been Wheatens, but we cannot be sure. What we can be sure about are the imports in 1946. They arrived by boat on November 23 and were consigned to Miss Lydia Vogel of West Springfield, Massachusetts.

The dogs were Fionn of Sonas (Cheerful Charlie ex Wheaten Lady) and Joyful Jessie (Dawson Lad ex Auchinleck). The next recorded imports were received by Mr. and Mrs. J.T. O'Brien of Washington, D.C., Holmenocks Hallinan (Holmenock's Highlander ex Ir. Ch. Handsome Hallmark of Holmenocks) and Holmenocks Hydova (Holmenocks Kismi Hardy ex Ir. Ch. Handsome Hallmark of Holmenocks).

Lydia showed Fionn and Jessie in the Miscellaneous Class at Westminster in 1947. This

The first imports to America in 1946 (left to right): Joyful Jessie and Fionn of Sonas.

was the first time Wheatens were exhibited in the United States as far as is known. Lydia continued to show and breed, but most of the dogs were sold as pets and only three dogs from her Berlyd line were ever registered with SCWTCA.

In *The Wheaten Years*, Maureen Holmes mentions two other dogs who were sent to the United States—Holmenocks Kismi Hardy (Glenguard Mourneside Firecrest ex Elegant Eileen of Holmenocks) and Anner Rose (Silver Whiskers ex Anner Bell) went to Indiana. Unlike Fionn of Sonas and Joyful Jessie, they were never registered with SCWTCA.

The next exported dogs whom she tells us about are Gads Hill, born in April, 1956 (Ir. Ch. Melauburn ex Ir. Ch. Holmenocks Herald) and a bitch Holmenocks Hallmark whelped in May, 1956 (Ir. Ch. Melauburn ex Homenocks Hilite). They were consigned to Mrs. Ann Hagan Howland, but eventually became the property of the Charles Arnolds of Connecticut.

Their call names were Liam and Maud. They produced a litter while the Howlands lived on Block Island. Those puppies were never registered and all were given to friends except one who went to the Arnolds. Liam later sired the historic July 4, 1962, litter out of Holmenocks Gramachree (Ir. Ch. Holmenocks Hartigan ex Griselda) that was owned by the O'Connor family that played such a large part in the development of the breed in the United States.

At about this same time, Margaret O'Connor found a picture of Fionn of Sonas in a magazine. Through the publisher she traced Lydia Vogel who referred her to the previously-mentioned Mr. O'Brien who referred her to Maureen Holmes in Ireland. The rest, as they say, is history.

In 1957, Holmenocks' Gramachree (Ir. Ch. Holmenocks Hartigan ex Griselda) became part of the O'Connor's Brooklyn, New York household. They called her Irish and Margaret showed her at the Staten Island KC show in 1961. Interest in

Ir. Ch. Kingdom Leader (Badger ex Molly) was one of the first Wheatens to become an Irish Champion.

Gramachree's Roderick Dhu CD with Dustin Hoffman on the set of the 1969 20th Century Fox film John and Mary. *"Max" was one of the first Wheatens in show business.*

World-renowned violinist Itzhak Perlman with a Wheaten puppy he purchased from Mary Ann Dallas.

Irish was so great that Margaret decided to locate other owners.

She finally found about a dozen other owners, including the Charles Arnolds and Louis and Ida Mallory. On March 17, 1962, a small group met and started the Soft Coated Wheaten Terrier Club of America to protect and preserve the Soft Coated Wheaten Terrier in the United States.

Margaret O'Connor used her public relations skills to promote Wheaten Terriers and started a Club newsletter which was named *Benchmarks*. She convinced Dan Kiedrowski, publisher of a fairly new monthly magazine, *Terrier Type,* to add a Wheaten column, which she wrote nearly every month until her untimely death in 1968. Her mother, Mrs. A. Cecelia O'Connor, continued the column through 1971.

THE O'CONNORS' CONTRIBUTION

The O'Connor family's unfailing devotion to the Soft Coated Wheaten Terrier is well documented. Margaret authored *How to Raise and Train a Soft Coated Wheaten Terrier* (Jersey City, NJ: TFH Publications, 1965). Her sister, Eileen Jackson and her brother, Tom, a Jesuit priest, showed Wheatens in both conformation and Obedience. Gramachree dogs were the first Wheatens to gain Obedience titles.

One of the most valuable contributions that Margaret O'Connor made was the creation of the SCWT Stud Book in 1965. She recorded the names of Wheatens, their pedigrees and their owners. These records were a requirement for AKC recognition which came in 1973. More than 1,100 dogs' records were listed when the Stud Book was submitted.

There is no doubt that the O'Connors did their part in working toward AKC recognition. Fr. Tom and his mother were active in the breed until after AKC acceptance. Rev. O'Connor still judges AKC Obedience Trials. He was a longtime member of AKC's Obedience Advisory Committee and judged the first Wheaten Specialty Obedience Trial in October 1996.

Many other Wheaten owners were important in the breed's early years in the United States. Their stories are found in Chapter 11, "Headliners." It took perseverance and a great deal of hard work on the part of all these pioneers to propel this Irish upstart into the exalted terrier mainstream—a place in which he is now most comfortable.

CHAPTER 3

Official Standard of the Soft Coated Wheaten Terrier with Interpretation

A breed Standard is a word picture of the ideal dog. It is the responsibility of the parent club of each breed to set forth the criteria by which all dogs of that breed will be judged. The Standard provided here was approved by the Soft Coated Wheaten Terrier Club of America on February 12, 1983. The italicized amplification is based on the visual presentation of the Standard produced by AKC in conjunction with the Soft Coated Wheaten Terrier Club of America. I served on the committee and helped to write the script. The video cassette is available from AKC and makes an excellent accompaniment to a study of the Standard.

In 1992, the SCWTCA produced its own illustrated Standard. While its amplification varies somewhat from the following, it must be remembered that interpretation of the Standard will always remain a subjective matter. For example, the term "moderate" can mean different things to different people. This is why different dogs win under different judges on different days. The *Illustrated Standard* is available from The Soft Coated Wheaten Terrier Club of America and is indispensable to every Wheaten owner's library.

GENERAL APPEARANCE—The Soft Coated Wheaten Terrier is a medium-sized, hardy, well-balanced sporting terrier, square in outline. He is distinguished by his soft, silky, gently waving coat of warm wheaten color and his particularly steady disposition. The breed requires moderation both in

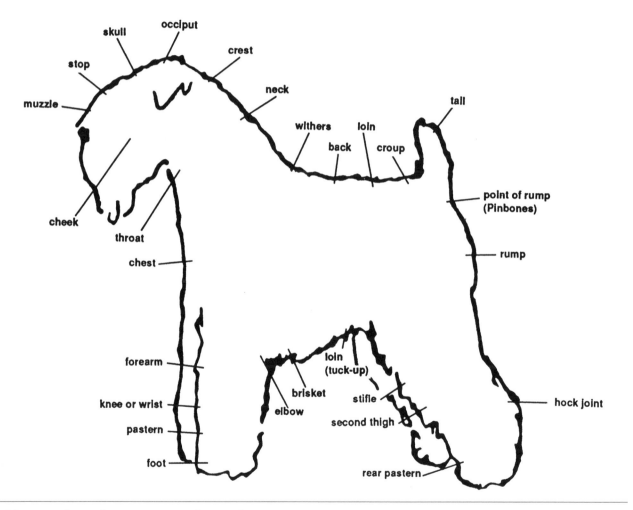

Wheaten outline indicating anatomical terminology.

structure and presentation, and any exaggerations are to be shunned. He should present the overall appearance of an alert and happy animal, graceful, strong and well coordinated.

The Soft Coated Wheaten Terrier's gently waving coat and easy nature impart a special image. While his Irish Terrier cousin is sleek, racy, and hard-coated and his Kerry Blue kin is more stylized and refined, the Wheaten is the casual country gentleman, more natural in trim and less aggressive in temperament. He combines the verve and zeal of the terrier with the steadiness of the working dog, remaining true to his heritage as a member of Ireland's terrier clan.

An example of a well-balanced Soft Coated Wheaten Terrier. (photo courtesy of American Kennel Club)

Three Irish cousins—the Soft Coated Wheaten Terrier (above), the Irish Terrier (lower right) and the Kerry Blue Terrier (lower left). (photo courtesy of American Kennel Club)

Note the position of a good-moving dog's shoulders when gaiting in relation to the handler's knee. (photo courtesy of American Kennel Club)

All parts of the dog, from the rectangular head to the set-on of tail, must present a picture of total balance. The term "well-balanced" is important, for it is used throughout the Standard. It is the basis of proper Wheaten structure.

SIZE, PROPORTION, SUBSTANCE—A dog shall be eighteen to nineteen inches at the withers, the ideal being eighteen and a half. A bitch shall be seventeen to eighteen inches at the withers, the ideal being seventeen and a half. *Major Faults:* Dogs under eighteen inches or over nineteen inches; bitches under seventeen inches or over eighteen inches. Any deviation must be penalized according to the degree of its severity. Square in outline. Hardy, well balanced. Dogs should weigh thirty-five to forty pounds; bitches thirty to thirty-five pounds.

Moderation is a key element of the proper Wheaten. The Wheaten is a sturdy, workmanlike dog and must be well boned, but never coarse in appearance. In general, bitches are more refined and finer in bone than dogs.

The Wheaten is a medium-sized dog, and although there is no size disqualification, breeders should make every effort to produce animals that are within the desired range of height and weight. It is easier to breed up in size than to retain moderation. As a guideline, the withers of an adult male of correct size usually line up just below the knee of an average human adult.

HEAD—Well balanced and in proportion to the body. Rectangular in appearance; moderately long. Powerful with no suggestion of coarseness.

The head should be moderately long, neither cloddy nor over refined and should be in proportion to the body. Picture it as one rectangle viewed from the front and two rectangles viewed from the side. The distance from the tip of the nose to the stop and from the stop to the back of the skull should be of equal length. There is a moderate stop. There should be sufficient length in each part so that the head has a rectangular rather than a square shape. The jaw must be powerful. There should not be chiseling under the eyes or prominent cheekbones, as these detract from the rectangular shape of the head.

Eyes dark reddish brown or brown, medium in size, slightly almond shaped and set fairly wide apart. Eye rims black. *Major Fault:* Anything approaching a yellow eye. *Ears* small to medium in size, breaking level with the skull and dropping slightly forward, the inside edge of the ear lying next to the cheek and pointing to the ground rather than to the eye. A hound ear or a high-breaking ear is not typical and should be *severely penalized.*

The eyes should be brown, not black, and never yellow. The dark, reddish-brown eye color predominates in the breed. The eyes should be slightly almond shaped, neither large and soulful nor small and hard-bitten. The eye rims must be black and in the mature dog, the black should extend onto the skin that surrounds the eye rims.

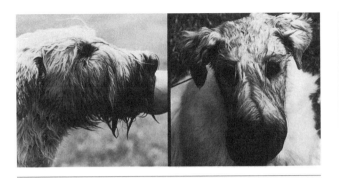

This wet down head clearly illustrates the head as two rectangles when viewed from the side. (photo courtesy of American Kennel Club)

Note how the dark eye trim extends onto the skin surrounding the eye. (photo courtesy of American Kennel Club)

This dog has a proper-sized, well-set ear. (photo courtesy of American Kennel Club)

The ears must not stand away from the head. A rose ear is objectionable. Houndy ears are also undesirable as are high set or button ears. The inside edge of the correct Wheaten ear should lie next to the cheek and point downward, not inward towards the eye.

Skull flat and clean between ears. Cheekbones not prominent. Defined stop. *Muzzle* powerful and strong, well filled below the eyes. No suggestion of snippiness. Skull and foreface of equal length. *Nose* black and large for size of dog. *Major Fault:* Any nose color other than solid black. Lips tight and black. *Teeth* large, clean and white; scissors or level bite. *Major Fault:* Undershot or overshot.

The large, black nose is one of the hallmarks of the breed. A brown or dudley nose is a serious fault. The nose must protrude beyond the fringe of hair that covers the face.

In either a scissors bite or a level bite the teeth must meet with no open space between the upper and lower incisors. Crooked or misaligned teeth should be discouraged.

Hound ears are considered faulty. (photo courtesy of
American Kennel Club)

Stand-away ears are objectionable. (photo courtesy of
American Kennel Club)

A rose ear—objectionable. (photo courtesy of American
Kennel Club)

Button ears. (photo courtesy of American
Kennel Club)

The large black nose protrudes beyond the fringe of hair on the muzzle. (photo courtesy of American Kennel Club)

Scissors bite; the inside of the upper incisors just engage the outside of the lower incisors. (photo courtesy of American Kennel Club)

Missing teeth should be penalized in accordance with the severity of the condition. Overshot or undershot mouths are major faults.

It must be noted that grooming plays an important role in the appearance of a Wheaten. Skillful trimming can enhance the appearance of a poor head just as poor trimming can spoil the appearance of a good head.

NECK, TOPLINE, BODY—*Neck* medium in length, clean and strong, not throaty. Carried proudly, it gradually widens, blending smoothly into the body.

Correct length of neck is important in achieving balance between head and body and providing a muscular base for efficient movement. The dog's neck should blend smoothly into the shoulder area. Here again, grooming can make a difference in the appearance of both set-on and

Level bite; the incisors meet tip to tip. (photo courtesy of American Kennel Club)

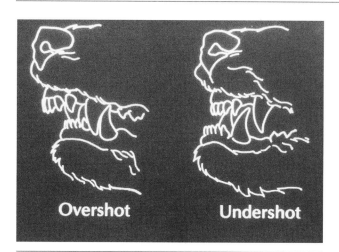

Overshot (left) and undershot bites. (photo courtesy of American Kennel Club)

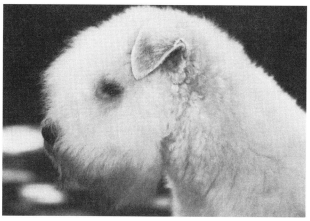

A poorly groomed head. (photo courtesy of American Kennel Club)

A well-groomed head. Here the eye is suggested, not exposed. (photo courtesy of American Kennel Club)

length of neck. While a longer neck may be esthetically more pleasing, it is not as strong as the more moderate length of neck called for in the Standard.

Back strong and level. *Body* compact; relatively short coupled. *Chest* is deep. *Ribs* are well sprung but without roundness. *Tail* is docked and well set on, carried gaily but never over the back.

Keep in mind that the Wheaten should "appear" square in outline, but is in fact slightly longer than tall. The rib cage is deep rather than round, and although well sprung, is not barrel shaped. The ribs should reach to the elbow at the brisket and should have sufficient width for heart and lungs. The ribs taper to a moderate tuck up; the loin is relatively short. The topline is level from withers to set on of tail with no dip, roach or sway in the back. Ideally, a well set-on tail should stand at a right angle to the topline and should be in balance with the rest of the dog. The tail should not be so long as to be level with the backskull, but rather it should be ½ to ⅔ the length of the neck. It should be neither too thick nor too spindly.

A moderate length neck blends smoothly into the dog's body. (photo courtesy of American Kennel Club)

Correct and incorrect rib structure. (photo courtesy of American Kennel Club)

Note compact body, short coupling, deep chest and well set-on tail. (photo courtesy of American Kennel Club)

This dog appears too long in body. (photo courtesy of American Kennel Club)

This dog is too tall. (photo courtesy of American Kennel Club)

FOREQUARTERS—*Shoulders* well-laid back, clean and smooth; well-knit. *Forelegs* straight and well-boned. All *dewclaws* should be removed. *Feet* are round and compact with good depth of pad. *Pads* black. *Nails* dark.

The shoulders should be close together at the withers. They should be well laid back to permit a long, free stride with plenty of reach in front. Upright shoulders or imbalance of the shoulder blade and the upper arm restrict front movement.

The forelegs form a straight line from elbow to foot. They should not turn in or out, and in movement should form a single column of support. Because of the coat, pasterns appear straight, but they should have a barely perceptible bend for shock absorption. They must be strong.

This dog has the correct proportion of height and body length. (photo courtesy of American Kennel Club)

Straight forelegs. (photo courtesy of American Kennel Club)

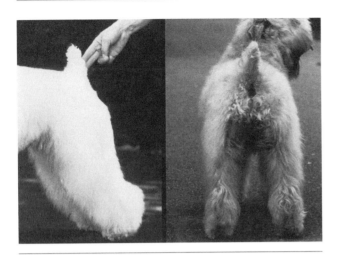

Well-bent stifles (left); well-let down hocks (right). (photo courtesy of American Kennel Club)

A proper round foot with good depth of pad. (photo courtesy of American Kennel Club)

HINDQUARTERS—*Hind legs* well-developed with well-bent *stifles* turning neither in nor out; *hocks* well-let down and parallel to each other. All *dewclaws* should be removed. The presence of dewclaws on the hind legs should be *penalized*. *Feet* are round and compact with good depth of pad. *Pads* black. *Nails* dark.

The hind legs are strong with rear angulation approximately the same as front angulation, which creates a balanced appearance and smooth gait. The distance from hock joint to ground is short and the bone is straight. The feet are firm, strong and round, not hare-footed or oval. A bad foot can sometimes be disguised by trimming, so a judge should check the shape of the foot in addition to checking the depth and color of the pads. An oval shape would indicate less depth and strength. Black nails are preferred, though tortoise is allowed. White nails are undesirable. Cow hocks, sickle hocks and open hocks are all incorrect and inhibit proper movement. Good rear angulation as well as correct hocks, are essential ingredients for good movement.

Faulty hocks interfere with proper movement. Shown here, from left, are cow hocks, sickle hocks and open hocks. (photo courtesy of American Kennel Club)

COAT—A distinguishing characteristic of the breed which sets the dog apart from all other terriers. An abundant single coat covering the entire body, legs and head; coat on the latter falls forward to shade the eyes. Texture soft and silky with a gentle wave. In both puppies and adolescents, the mature wavy coat is generally not yet evident. *Major Faults:* Woolly or harsh, crisp or cottony, curly or standaway coat; in the adult, a straight coat is also objectionable.

Understanding and defining proper Wheaten coat has caused more problems than any other aspect of the breed. It is vital to realize that the coat goes through various stages during the dog's life. The adult Wheaten has a single coat which is soft, silky and shiny. It should fall in loose waves or curls. There should be no tendency to a woolly or wiry texture. Puppies carry a soft, plush, dense coat with intense, rich color. As the Wheaten approaches adolescence his coat often displays less color and the texture will be a mixture of fine puppy hair and more heavily textured adult coat.

After the age of two, the warm wheaten color and gentle wave should be evident. The adult coat is deeper colored than that of the adolescent, wavier and less dense. It lies closer to the body in loose waves. The difference is analogous to comparing the texture of a human child's hair to human adult hair. Although proper coat is important, it must be remembered that color, quality, texture and condition of the coat is only one factor in judging the entire dog. It should be given neither more nor less attention than coat in any other breed.

PRESENTATION—For show purposes, the Wheaten is presented to show a terrier outline, but coat must be of sufficient length to flow when the dog is in motion. The coat must never be clipped or plucked. Sharp contrasts or stylizations must be avoided. Head coat should be blended to present a rectangular outline. Eyes should be indicated but never fully

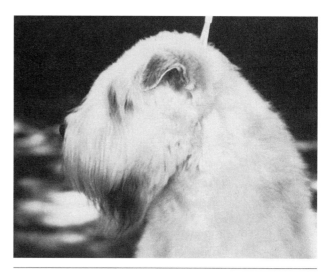

Head coat falls so that it shades the eyes. (photo courtesy of American Kennel Club)

The dog in the background has a curly, woolly coat. The dog in the foreground has a proper coat. (photo courtesy of American Kennel Club)

exposed. Ears should be relieved of fringe, but not taken down to the leather. Sufficient coat must be left on skull, cheeks, neck and tail to balance the

Plush, deeply colored puppy coat. (photo courtesy of American Kennel Club)

A proper adult coat. (photo courtesy of American Kennel Club)

Lighter-colored adolescent coat. (photo courtesy of American Kennel Club)

The Soft Coated Wheaten Terrier should always appear stylish, neat and natural in both ring and home. (photo courtesy of American Kennel Club)

proper length of body coat. *Dogs that are overly trimmed shall be severely penalized.*

The Wheaten should be presented in a more natural manner than most other terriers. Too much trimming must be penalized in the show ring. The head should be tidied to demonstrate the rectangular outline, thinning where needed to achieve a clean appearance. Eyes must not be exposed.

The body coat is tipped and thinned to tidy the stray hairs and to smooth out areas of dense growth while following the outline of the dog. Blending is critical in order to avoid visible trim lines. The finished dog should look stylish and neat, but natural.

Shaded and unshaded ears and muzzles. Both are acceptable. (photo courtesy of American Kennel Club)

AUTHOR'S COMMENT: More and more Wheatens being shown are so stylized that they are beginning to look like blonde Kerries with topknots like Dandie Dinmonts. The falls resemble visors. Exposed eyes really bother me. Until breeders, exhibitors and judges start to follow the Standard, the trimming will only become more extreme. We have superb guidelines in the SCWTCA *Illustrated Standard.* It is time to return to the kind of trimming that is unique to the Wheaten and is "stylish, neat and natural." Judges need to recognize that good grooming skills can hide a multitude of sins and conversely, poor trimming can detract from a well-constructed animal. Thorough manual examination is a must and should be combined with careful study of the dog's movement.

COLOR—Any shade of wheaten. Upon close examination, occasional red, white or black guard hairs may be found. However, the overall coloring must be clearly wheaten with no evidence of any other color except on ears and muzzle where blue-gray shading is sometimes present. *Major Fault:* Any color save wheaten.

Correct color is any shade of wheaten from pale blonde to warm honey. There should be no other color anywhere except for blue shading on ears and muzzle which is fairly common but does not occur on all dogs. Either way is acceptable. Coat color changes throughout the life of the dog, but the Wheaten Terrier is always some shade of blonde. The adult Wheaten should not be expected to carry the intense color of puppy coat nor must he ever appear gray, grizzle or white.

PUPPIES AND ADOLESCENTS—Puppies under a year may carry deeper coloring and occasional black tipping. The adolescent, under two years, is often quite light in color, but must never be white or carry gray other than on ears and muzzle. However, by two years of age, the proper wheaten color should be obvious.

GAIT—Gait is free, graceful and lively with good reach in front and strong drive behind. Front and rear feet turn neither in nor out. Dogs who fail to keep their tails erect when moving should be *severely penalized.*

Correct assembly and balance of front and rear will enable the dog to move smoothly and efficiently. The Wheaten is a working terrier and thus requires reach in front and drive behind, permitting the dog to cover maximum ground with minimum effort.

Viewed in profile when moving, the Wheaten should look as though only the legs are moving. The body and topline should be carried along smoothly, neither bouncing nor rolling. He will tend to single track at faster speeds, but this should not be confused with moving too close behind or weaving or crossing in front.

An efficient, balanced gait is one which will enable the dog to perform the tasks for which he was bred. Good front movement depends on a correct and balanced front assembly. The rear movement should be powerful with the legs forming a single column of support from hip to ground.

TEMPERAMENT—The Wheaten is a happy, steady dog and shows himself gaily with an air of self-confidence. He is alert and exhibits interest in his surroundings; exhibits less aggressiveness than is some-times encouraged in other terriers. *Major Fault:* Timid or overly aggressive dogs.

The Wheaten is steady, merry and full of fun, but should stand his ground when he is pro-voked. He should give evidence of a happy, stable temperament, never surly, timid or aggressive.

An example of good reach and drive. (photo courtesy of American Kennel Club)

A group of Wheatens showing interest in each other but not aggressive-ness. (photo courtesy of American Kennel Club)

Carried gaily erect, the Wheaten tail is an indicator of his happy nature.

SUMMARY

This brief discussion of the Soft Coated Wheaten Terrier Standard is meant to provide some guidelines for breeders and judges. It is incumbent upon those who judge the breed to realize that the dogs to whom they award championship points will become the breeding stock of the future. Therefore, judges have a great influence on how the Soft Coated Wheaten Terrier develops and changes. However, the ultimate responsibility of maintaining breed type rests with the breeders. There will always be those who will breed to the day's top winner regardless of whether he complements a bitch or not. In the long run, it is the breeder who has a well-planned breeding program who will consistently produce sound, healthy and typey Wheatens.

Interpretation of a breed Standard is a subjective process as was observed earlier in this chapter. By studying the SCWTCA's *Illustrated Standard*, the AKC Standard video, pictures and the dogs themselves, breeders and judges will be better able to continue the search for the "ideal" Soft Coated Wheaten Terrier as set forth in the official Standard.

(photo © John Ashbey)

CHAPTER 4

Finding the Right Wheaten

I f you have decided that you are willing to accept the responsibility of caring for a Soft Coated Wheaten Terrier and all that goes with it, finding the dog of your dreams is the next logical step. The first thing to do is locate a breeder in whom you have confidence. If you are determined to get a puppy or young adult, the breeder route is what you need to follow. You might consider taking a rescue Wheaten. There is more on this very important issue later in this chapter.

LOCATING A BREEDER

SCWTCA members are prohibited by their Code of Ethics from supplying dogs for resale by a third party. Wheatens sold in retail establishments are usually bred and raised by commercial breeders as a cash crop. These sellers are likely to have no idea about Wheaten care and grooming. If you have already purchased a dog from such a source, do not despair. Try to locate a Wheaten club or other Wheaten owners in your area and develop a support system. You can also obtain SCWTCA publications directly from the parent club.

Should you answer a newspaper advertisement, be sure to find out whether the person is a member of the national club or of a local club. Ask if he shows his dogs and whether his dogs have attained any AKC titles in conformation, performance or both. Active involvement in a Wheaten club is often a good indication that a person has more than a monetary interest in breeding dogs.

Very often, newspaper advertisers are "backyard breeders" who produce one or two litters a year. While these dogs may be "home raised" their breeders often lack knowledge of pedigrees and Wheaten health problems and may lack the hobby breeder's dedication to breed improvement.

As puppy buyers become more sophisticated regarding the best place to buy a dog, commercial breeders sometimes sell puppies through individuals. The puppies are advertised as being "home bred." The seller will often claim that he is selling the dogs for a relative who lives in a rural area where the market is poor. The mother of the litter is almost never present. Imported litters are often sold this way also. Keep in mind that the reputable hobby breeder rarely advertises in the local newspaper. Like backyard breeders, those who sell puppies for Aunt Susie usually lack any knowledge of Wheaten care.

Dog shows are good places to see Wheatens and to meet breeders. As a courtesy, don't approach owners or handlers just as they are about to enter the show ring. Wait until the dog is finished being shown before initiating a conversation. Dog exhibitors love to talk about their breed, and if they do not have puppies, they often know who is expecting puppies and when, and who currently has puppies for sale.

AKC will supply you with the address of the parent club secretary who will, in turn, send you a list of member-breeders. These people subscribe to the SCWTCA Code of Ethics. Both AKC and the SCWTCA have Internet Web sites where you can gather additional information.(See Appendix A.)

When you make contact with the AKC, ask also for the address of a Specialty club in your area. Clubs are an excellent source of information about Wheatens. They also offer an opportunity to meet other Wheaten owners and learn more about the breed on a personal level.

Be prepared to wait for the dog you want. Your breeder may not have a dog available when you are ready. Remember, you will have your dog for a long time, so be patient and you will end up with the right puppy.

Hullabaloo in a New York Minute and Ch. McLaren's Whisper My Name posing for the camera on a visit to the American Kennel Club Library. The world-famous library is the ideal resource for information on all dog breeds, dog sports and general dog-related subjects as well as the addresses of breed clubs. (photo by Sally Sotirovich)

Breeders want to find good homes for their dogs. They will ask you many questions about your lifestyle. Most will require that if you cannot keep the dog, you return it to them. It is usual for a breeder to ask you to sign an agreement that covers certain conditions of sale. These can include showing, spaying/neutering, stud rights and leasing for breeding, among other possibilities. Just be sure that everything mutually agreeable to you and the breeder is in writing. A year after you get your Wheaten, you or the breeder may honestly not remember a particular term of an oral agreement. Putting everything on paper is always the fairest and most prudent course for the protection of both parties to any transaction of this kind.

This is a sight you are likely to see on a visit to the breeder. (photo by Leigh Michel)

Most SCWTCA member breeders use a standard contract that clearly describes the dog being sold and the obligations of both buyer and seller. This contract requires that the dog be returned to the breeder if the new owner is unable to keep it. (Most member-breeders accept responsibility for the dogs they breed for the life of the animal.) This contract also requires that dogs sold as pets must be spayed or neutered.

When you go to see the puppies, don't be surprised to see dark brown or reddish balls of fur. The color will lighten with age. Dark shading often remains on the ears and muzzle. Some Wheatens are born very light and breeders consider these to be "pet quality," especially if they lack black pigment on the nose, eye rims and pads.

The puppies should be lively and bright-eyed. They should be curious about you and want to be picked up. There will be some characteristic "aroma of puppy" but you should get a general impression of cleanliness. Don't be disconcerted if the mother dog seems a bit aggressive. Her instincts tell her to protect her young. You may have to meet her in another room to get a true impression of her temperament.

Look for signs that the puppies are not well cared for: really long nails, unkempt coats, runny eyes and distended bellies. A responsible breeder keeps her puppies clean and well fed. She sees that they have veterinary care as needed.

Do not be turned off by a breeder referring to a dog as being of "pet quality." This only means that the dog is not a likely show prospect. The dog

This type of puppy pen is ideal for even a large litter. (photo by Sally Sotirovich)

proposition in terms of time, effort and money. Make your position clear and stick with it.

Don't be misled by what you may have heard about "pick of the litter." There is really no such thing. If the breeder plans to keep a puppy as a show prospect, you can be sure that she will keep the one she considers the best. You will have to rely on the breeder's judgment to a great extent. She has lived with those puppies since they were born. Based on previous experience, she has a pretty good idea which one will fit best with you and your family.

may lack pigment, or have some other physical feature that makes him less desirable as a show dog. Breeders make these decisions based on their familiarity with the breed Standard and their experience with how previous litters they have bred grew on. If what you want is a lovely companion, and you are comfortable with the breeder, by all means, buy the puppy.

By the same token, you might question a breeder who claims that every pup in the litter is a "show prospect." Be careful that your desire to own a Wheaten does not overwhelm your common sense. If you truly don't wish to show, don't let yourself get talked into it. Showing a dog to its conformation championship is a demanding

THE BREEDER'S OBLIGATIONS

Your breeder should provide you with a list of detailed instructions for feeding and caring for the puppy. Most will give you a small supply of the food that the puppy has been eating. It is best to discuss what the puppy is eating well ahead of the time you will bring him home so that you can have the proper food on hand when he becomes your dog.

The other documents that should come with the puppy are a health record listing the shots the puppy has had, a pedigree or family tree, and an application to register the dog with the AKC. This form is what most people mean when they refer to "papers." If it is properly completed and submitted with the fee to AKC, in about three weeks you will receive a registration certificate. AKC requires a seller to provide a bill of sale identifying the dog. Any agreement to withhold papers must be in writing.

AKC offers breeders the option of a Limited Registration category for individual puppies. Offspring of a dog with Limited Registration cannot be registered with AKC. This program helps a breeder keep control of her breeding program. A dog with a Limited Registration can participate in all AKC licensed events except conformation competition at an AKC licensed show. The breeder of record is the only person who can rescind the Limited Registration designation later if she chooses. This could happen if a puppy developed into a better specimen than the breeder expected. If your breeder uses this type of registration, and the puppy you buy is so registered, this fact should be prominently noted in writing on the bill of sale or contract.

Some breeders will hold the application form for a week or ten days. This allows a reasonable

As long as weather permits, a safely fenced run is a great place for puppies. This litter is very friendly to strangers, as it has been well socialized at the right time. (photo by Sally Sotirovich)

time period in which you take the puppy to your own veterinarian to find out if he is as the breeder described him. It also saves paperwork in case you change your mind and decide to return the puppy and allows time for your check to clear. It is not pleasant for a breeder to deliver a dog and then have a check bounce and be left with neither dog nor money. Most transactions occurring in the dog game are built on good faith. Indeed, almost all breeders and buyers are total strangers before the latter seeks out the former. If you have done your homework and enjoy a good rapport with your breeder, chances are it will be a long and pleasant relationship.

ACQUIRING AN OLDER WHEATEN

Some people may wish to get an older dog rather than a puppy. Breeders occasionally have mature dogs available whom they wish to place. There is nothing wrong with these dogs; they may no longer be needed in the breeding program or they may have finished their championships and will no longer be shown. Often, the caring breeder would prefer to see these dogs happily living in pet homes rather than living out their lives as inactive members of a breeding/showing group. If you select that option, remember the adult dog's basic personality is already set. You will probably have to do some retraining, and it may take some time before the close bonding you want takes place. Carol Benjamin's book, *Second-Hand Dog* (New York: Howell Book House, 1988), has helpful suggestions and hints for dealing with this situation. Even an abused Wheaten will respond to love and trust and most can usually be rehabilitated with love, patience and thoughtful training.

Occasionally, a Wheaten ends up in a shelter. They are always adopted very quickly. In our local rescue network, by the time we learn that a Wheaten is in a shelter, the animal is usually in his new home. While people involved with rescue activities try to maintain communication with animal shelters, it is not always successful. At the very least, we ask them to have the new owners contact us for any support we can provide.

RESCUE DOGS

Like other national breed clubs, SCWTCA has a rescue program. Most local clubs also provide this service. AKC has a list of breed rescue contacts. A rescue dog is not a way to get a "free or cheap" pet. Keep in mind that when people surrender a dog to the rescue committee, there is a reason for it. Some of these reasons, like illness, divorce or a family move, are quite legitimate. Animal behavior problems and the owner's unwillingness to keep the dog play a significant role when contact is made with the rescue committee. Very often these dogs were impulse purchases from persons other than established breeders. Typically, the dogs are young, not groomed, often not housebroken and poorly trained. Sometimes the rescue contact is able to offer a solution to the problem that is causing the owner to want to give up the dog. This can be as simple as recommending crate training, offering a grooming demonstration or referring the owner to a reliable trainer.

Aggressive dogs are not accepted into rescue programs. Owners are advised to have such animals euthanized. When rescue does take a dog, it is put in a foster home or kennel and evaluated for at least two weeks before being placed in a new home. Any health problems are treated as necessary and the animal is neutered/spayed. Prospective owners are carefully screened. The new owner must agree to return the dog to the rescue if the adoption does not work.

If you decide to seek a rescue dog, you will be sent an application to adopt which must be completed and returned to rescue. It will be filed and you will be notified when a suitable animal is available. There are pros and cons to getting a rescue dog. It is probably less expensive than getting a young puppy from a breeder, but bonding may take longer. Some latent behavior problems may remain. By and large, thanks to the inherent adaptability of the Wheaten and its basic good nature, most of SCWTCA's rescue efforts are successful.

But whether you are adopting an older dog or buying a brand new puppy, it behooves you to do your homework and exercise lots of care. You are making a long-term commitment and you want it to bring you joy and pleasure, not problems and regrets. Do your homework first, and then, when you see the right dog for you, you can let a little emotion and impulse creep into your decision.

(photo © Marcie Grannick)

CHAPTER 5

Living with Your Wheaten

Living happily with your Wheaten requires a willingness to spend time and effort training your dog. The training starts when you bring your puppy home. The puppy is father to the grown dog. How you treat your puppy will affect his adult behavior.

Trainers once believed that, beyond housetraining, a dog had to be at least six months old before it could be trained. This was probably a holdover from the days when dogs actually hunted. In recent years, extensive study has been conducted in the field of animal behavior, and the current wisdom is that puppies can and should be trained to sit, stay, heel and come at an early age. This can start as early as seven or eight weeks.

This is not a training manual, so I will just touch on some key aspects of training that the new Wheaten owner needs to know. As a matter of fact, while I have taken my own dogs through Obedience courses, I have never actually competed in the Obedience ring myself. This was not the fault of my dogs. *Training a dog without training his owner is not enough.* There are many new techniques and training aids available, and it is very important that you, as a dog owner, seek information about them. A list of sources appears in Appendix A. My purpose is to outline specific areas that need special attention because we are dealing with Soft Coated Wheaten Terriers and to acquaint new owners with the responsibility that goes with dog ownership.

One of the best things to do with a young puppy is to enroll him in a "Kindergarten Puppy Training Class." The concept was pioneered by Dr. Ian Dunbar. (His booklet and video are excellent training tools.) Wheatens respond better to more formal obedience work when they are beyond the adolescent stage. All training should be firm and consistent, not rough.

HOUSETRAINING

Housetraining is the generally accepted term that means teaching your dog that inside your house is not the place for him to relieve himself. An unclean dog often ends up badly, so this aspect of your dog's training should be your top priority. Dogs are innately hygienic. They do not like to eliminate close to where they eat and sleep. However, if there is a door or barrier blocking a suitable place, the dog has no choice but to use his room. Therefore, you must be there to take him to the place you have chosen as his toilet. Dogs purchased from pet shops may be used to eliminating in their crates. It will be difficult to

Many Wheatens love to play in water. (photo by Judy Mohr)

break this habit, but it can be done.

Housetraining is easier if you establish a routine for feeding and walking. A dog needs to eliminate when he wakes and after he eats. A puppy of less than six months of age does not have the physical capacity to last more than a few hours without relieving himself.

A crate is an excellent aid to housetraining. Use of a crate is not cruel as is often wrongly supposed. Dogs are den animals. They need a place of their own. People who resist the use of crates are mistakenly projecting their own needs and fears onto their dogs. A crate provides a safe haven for your puppy when you are not at home. You may even wish to feed your dog in his crate. This is a must for anyone who owns more than one dog. Conscientious breeders accustom their puppies to a crate before they are sold. A crate is essential for traveling with your dog, even to the veterinarian or any other short trips. Never use a crate as punishment, but only as a place with positive associations for your Wheaten.

Ch. McClaren's Clean Sweep, known as Hoover, is a contented Wheaten enjoying his owner Mary Ann Havron's affection. (photo by Sally Sotirovich)

The crate needs to be large enough to comfortably accommodate an adult dog. While your dog is small, you can block off part of his crate and, as he grows, increase the space as required. The idea is to avoid the possibility of his eliminating in the crate. Do not leave a puppy under four months of age in his crate for more than an hour at a time.

When you are present to watch him, leave the crate door open so the dog can go in and out. If he sniffs, squats, circles or gives any indication he is ready to urinate, take him immediately outside to the place you wish him to use. Praise him when he performs as required. If you use a unique word or phrase while your dog is eliminating, he will eventually connect the word with the act and will perform on command. Always use the same words and don't use them for any other situation or command. Praise him extravagantly for "getting it right."

Whether or not to "paper" train a puppy is a matter on which breeders disagree. It certainly has its place in an urban environment. It is not easy to get a very young puppy out an apartment door, into the elevator and out to the curb in time to prevent an accident. It is probably easier to put down newspapers—but do this only in a small area, please. When the dog has adequate bladder and bowel control, he can make the transition to the outdoors. Always clean up after your dog. It is simple and convenient to carry plastic sandwich bags with you whenever you walk your dog. One of my pet peeves is people who don't clean up after their dogs. I have been known to hand them a sandwich bag and say politely, "Here, I always carry a spare."

The critical elements of housetraining are as follows: a crate or confined area, an established routine (don't switch on weekends just so you can sleep a little longer) and lots of praise. When the puppy is ready for a nap, put him in his crate and shut and fasten the door. Don't let him out if he fusses, or you will lose your status as pack leader. When your puppy wakes, take him right out to his "spot" and remember to praise him for doing as he should.

Your new puppy will probably eat three times a day and therefore will need to be taken to his "toilet" more often and certainly after each meal. While housetraining, it might help to ration water. Before bed you can offer ice cubes, as they will

Wheatens are happiest when doing things with their owners. (photo by Guy and Susan Lima)

quench his thirst while not filling his bladder. You may wish to keep your puppy and his crate in your bedroom with you for a few nights until he really feels at home. If you can't do this, leave a radio playing for him. Remember, he will become accustomed to whatever routine you set. You make the rules. Don't give in to his complaints. The effort spent in these early weeks is well worth it when the result is a clean, happy Wheaten for life.

JUMPING AND LEASH PULLING

Wheatens jump up when they greet people. Most are capable of leaping three or four feet straight off the ground to give an enthusiastic, wet kiss to whomever they deem deserving. If not halted at a young age, jumping can become a serious problem and threatens the safety of people. There are many suggestions to stop this serious problem. One of the most sensible that I have found is given in William E. Campbell's *Owner's Guide to Better Behavior in Dogs and Cats*. He tells us that dogs jump up to a person's face to smell the breath. This is generally a friendly gesture, but if your dog injures someone in his exuberance, friendliness is quite irrelevant. Problem jumping starts when owners encourage a puppy to jump up and play. The dog cannot discriminate between acceptable and unacceptable jumping. The first step is to stop this kind of play.

Teaching your dog to sit before he gets any attention from you, (including greeting, petting or feeding) is the key to solving the jumping problem. The technique can be used in other training situations as well.

You will need to use the correct collar when you are training. A "choke" collar or chain is required. This is a collar that tightens when it is pulled and makes the necessary correction. It must be put on properly or it won't work. NEVER leave a choke collar on a dog unless he is being trained. It could catch on something and strangle the dog. The best chain collar for your Wheaten is a fine-linked metal "snake" chain. This type will not wear the neck coat away. I use a rolled nylon choke for routine walks and the chain for training. (My dog sometimes "heels" automatically when she's wearing it.)

Wheatens take justifiable delight in their great athletic abilities. (photo by Sue Poulin)

When the dog sits, praise him from a crouching position by scratching his chest. Make the praise sufficient to reward your dog without overly exciting him. Practice this procedure until the sit is automatic. Remember to make your dog work for whatever you give him. Repeat the exercise several times until the dog understands what you want. Eventually, he will learn to sit on command whether he is on a lead or not.

It is a pleasure to walk a dog who stays by your side on a loose lead. Wheatens are notorious leash-pullers. Their necks are so strong and their heavy coats are so thick that normal leash corrections don't seem to work. When they forge ahead, it is difficult to keep the collar up close behind the ears where it does the most good in a correction.

A Wheaten puppy with some safe play toys. (photo by Mel Brooks)

There are nearly as many methods of teaching sit as there are trainers. One of the clearest I've found is the one Brian Kilcommons recommends in his book, *Good Owners, Great Dogs.* This version is a bit condensed. Put the chain collar and lead on your dog and stand with him on your left side. Hold the leash in your right hand with even tension. Reach down with your left hand, forming a U with your thumb and fingers. Press down gently just in front of the dog's hip bones, give the "sit" command and guide the dog into position.

If allowed, Wheatens will make your best furniture part of their territory. (photo by P. Hauschildt and C. Noel)

One way to try to teach a Wheaten to walk on a loose lead is to constantly change directions until he will stay close to your left knee and pay attention to you. A squeaky toy or treat may help. You will note that I said "try" to teach. Many people are successful in getting their dog to walk nicely on a loose lead. Many Wheatens do achieve Obedience titles. But don't get discouraged if you meet too much resistance. I myself have found this training to be difficult, and the best advice I can give is to go to an Obedience class and practice, practice, practice.

There are other things that you have to teach your dog to make him a good canine citizen: coming when called, staying in one place and lying down. Techniques for teaching these skills can be found in many books and on videocassettes. Any basic Obedience course will include these exercises. Take the time to teach your dog essential good manners. You will both be better for it. Remember, as one of my breeder friends says, Wheatens are best trained with a firm hand in a velvet glove.

(photo © Mary Lou Lafler)

CHAPTER 6

Keeping Your Soft Coated Wheaten Terrier Happy and Healthy

This chapter is primarily directed at the typical one-Wheaten family. For potential owners, knowing what needs to be done to keep a Soft Coated Wheaten Terrier healthy and looking his best can be a major factor in deciding whether or not they want to make the commitment to providing the special care a Wheaten needs. For most owners, the pleasure of owning a clean, well-kept Wheaten is more than ample reward for the effort required.

We are fortunate to live in a time when new medical treatments and health maintenance methods appear and improve almost by the minute. But your dog's basic health needs stay the same. Keeping your Wheaten healthy and comfortable means providing an adequate, nutritious diet, regular exercise and routine grooming. The Wheaten is a characteristically healthy, hardy animal and, in most cases, an annual visit to the veterinarian to update vaccinations is all that an adult dog needs.

YOU AND YOUR VETERINARIAN

As soon as you know when you are bringing your puppy home, make an appointment with a veterinarian. This should be within one or two days from the time you get your dog. Choosing a veterinarian is important and may prove to be among the most critical factors in your dog's life. Ask other dog owners in your local area for references. You may have to try more than one vet before you find one in whom you have confidence. You will have a long relationship with this person and you should be as comfortable with a veterinarian as you are with your own personal physician. It is also a good idea to locate a nearby emergency veterinary service. These clinics are usually open when your regular vet does not have hours—on evenings, weekends and holidays.

Whenever you take your puppy to the vet for routine matters, leave him in your car until the doctor is ready to see you. Try to find someone to go with you to stay with the youngster. There is every possibility that sick animals will be present in the waiting room and you don't need to expose your healthy animal to possible infection. At your first visit, bring any health records (shots, wormings) that your breeder has given you. Expect the doctor to examine your puppy thoroughly. He should check ears, eyes, heart, lungs and abdomen. He will most likely request a stool sample. If parasites are present, the doctor will prescribe the appropriate medicine. It is not unusual for a young puppy to have round-worms. Most breeders worm their puppies before they go the their new homes. By the age of one year, your Wheaten should have received all the inoculations he needs and will then only require annual booster shots.

The dog will receive a program of shots over a period of months to protect him from distemper, hepatitis and

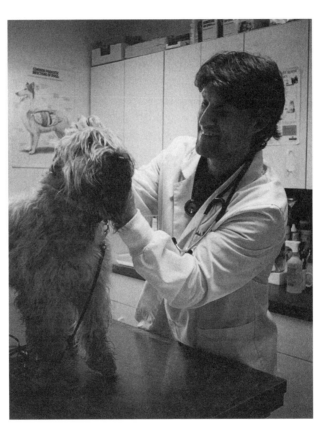

The author's Kate with her veterinarian, Dr. Robert Hendrickson. It is important to find a caring, competent vet with whom you feel at ease. Make sure your vet has all the protocols for anesthesia regarding Wheatens, protein losing enteropathy (PLE) and protein losing nephropathy (PLN) in his files. (photo by Allan Vesley)

leptospirosis. The doctor may also administer shots for parvo, a gastrointestinal virus. Of late, there is some controversy about giving all the shots at one time in one combined vaccine. Some research indicates that there is a possible link between combined vaccination and subsequent kidney problems.

Rabies is a fatal infectious disease affecting animals and humans. In some parts of the United States it is on the rise among wild animals such as skunks and raccoons. If you should see a wild animal acting strangely, don't touch it; notify your local animal control authority and don't let your dog near it. Fortunately, rabies vaccines provide complete protection for your dog. In many communities vaccination is required in order to obtain a dog license. Rabies vaccine was formerly given after the age of six months. Current vaccines can be given much earlier and some last for three years.

At some point in time, your Wheaten may need to have surgery. Obviously, if you do not plan to breed, spaying or neutering will be one such occasion. Please be advised that, like sight hounds, some Wheatens have a sensitivity to anesthesia. Please see the information regarding anesthesia in Appendix D and make a copy of the guidelines a part of your dog's medical records.

ROUTINE MAINTENANCE

Once your puppy has been given a clean bill of health, it is up to you to keep him that way by

This young Wheaten is the picture of health and seems happy with this safe toy. (photo by Gay Dunlap)

providing an adequate diet, regular exercise and sufficient grooming that is carried out on a regular schedule. The first thing to do is to learn what is normal for your dog. A typical Wheaten is lively and alert. Most also have a good appetite. His eyes are clear and bright. His gums and tongue are pink and his nose is moist and cool. If these obvious signs of good health change, it is time to investigate.

Observe your dog's behavior carefully. Be aware of changes that might indicate the presence of internal parasites. If he sleeps more than usual or if he is lethargic, it is likely that your dog needs to see the veterinarian. Any time you think your Wheaten may be ill, the first thing you must do, if you suspect he has a fever, is to take his temperature using a rectal thermometer. The normal temperature for a dog is about 101.5°F. If it is 104°F or higher, call your vet or emergency clinic. Just as a human mother almost instinctively knows when her infant is not up to par, dog owners need to accustom themselves to recognizing when their animals appear in any way off color.

Some things need to be checked almost daily. Pay attention to your dog's feet. Cut the hair between the pads frequently to keep the feet tightly compact and springy. Small stones and twigs can get caught in the hair and cause pain. Use blunt-nosed scissors. Accustom your puppy to having his feet handled even before much hair grows there.

Wheaten nails grow rapidly. If the your dog's nails click when he walks on a hard floor, the nails are too long. Some dogs wear their nails down naturally. For instance, a dog who is walked on concrete or who uses a cement surfaced run regularly will not need as much nail trimming as a dog who is rarely exposed to hard surfaces. If the nails get too long, the toes tend to spread and the pasterns weaken.

There is a vein, called the quick, running through each of the dog's nails. If the nails are cut or filed frequently and kept short, this vein recedes which helps keep the feet tight and strong. The quick will bleed if it is cut, so have some kind of styptic powder at hand when trimming nails—just in case. I cannot stress too strongly the importance of doing nails weekly. (See the diagrams for instructions.)

Examine your dog's ears often, especially if you notice frequent head shaking. Remove excess hair from the ear canal using your fingers or a hemostat. Trim hair around the opening of the ear as well as on the underside of the ear flap. This lightens the ear flap and permits the flow of air. You may also use an ear cleaning liquid to wipe away dirt or wax from the ear. See your veterinarian if you detect an odor or if a brown waxy accumulation is present. This is a sign of infection and needs professional attention before it develops into a painful chronic condition.

Eyes tear and matter accumulates. Regular, gentle cleaning with a moist cotton ball should prevent staining or at least keep it to a minimum.

PARASITES

The most common parasites affecting dogs are fleas, ticks and worms. In some areas mites can also be a problem. Because it is longhaired, a Soft Coated Wheaten Terrier needs more careful examination to detect the presence of external parasites than smooth coated dogs or dogs with less profuse coats.

Fleas

There is a plethora of new products for treatment of fleas on the market. Many are only available from veterinarians. Fleas are insidious pests that occur throughout the world. They transmit disease and make your dog's life miserable and can also infest humans.

Fleas live in the environment, not on your dog. The adults bite their host, drawing blood for nourishment, and then lay eggs that hatch into larvae. These larvae pupate and develop into adults that bite your dog and repeat the cycle. In order to solve a flea problem, you must treat the environs of

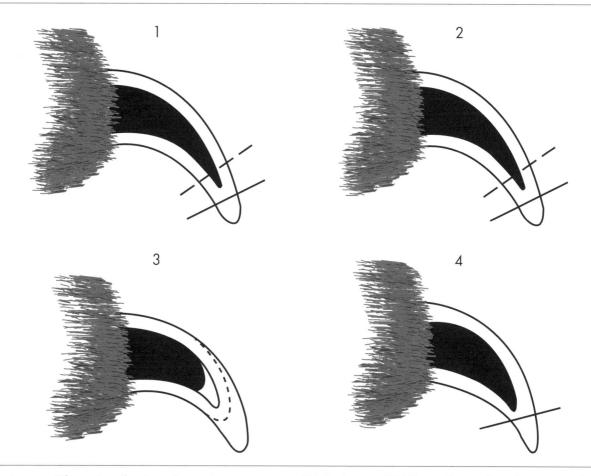

Keeping your Wheaten's nails trimmed is an important aspect of his basic care. #1) When nails are allowed to grow too long, as here, the "quick," or blood supply, will also grow long and cutting nails without bleeding is difficult. If cut at the bottom line, the quick will not bleed, but the nail will remain too long. If cut at the top line, there will be slight bleeding and the quick will begin to recede. #2) and #3) As the nail is gradually worked back, the quick becomes shorter and trimming is less likely to result in bleeding. #4) This is the angle at which nails should be trimmed. The point at which they are trimmed will vary with overall length of the shortened quicks.

your home, especially where the dog sleeps. Treat the outdoors and treat the dog as well.

Many Wheatens are susceptible to flea bite allergy which manifests itself in hot spots—red, inflamed areas with hair loss. It is important to act at the first sign of fleas. Consult your veterinarian for products that he considers safe and effective. Some of the new products are formulated to act on the different stages of a flea's life cycle. They are not insecticides like other flea-killing powders and sprays and dips. Some products kill adult fleas before they can reproduce. These are applied topically once a month and at least one brand kills ticks also. There is a tablet in which the active ingredient prevents flea eggs from hatching. It should be given once a month. There is another once a month tablet that works against fleas, heartworm, hookworm and whipworm. Your veterinarian can prescribe what is best for your Wheaten in your area.

Ticks

Like fleas, ticks have a complex life cycle. Only a few days are spent on the host animal. Some carry Rocky Mountain spotted fever. The minute deer tick spreads Lyme disease to people and to dogs. Both male and female ticks bite the host animal, but it is the female that attaches itself and becomes engorged with blood. To remove a tick that is attached to your dog, apply a few drops of alcohol to the spot. Then take a tweezer or forceps and grab the tick close to the point of attachment and twist in a counter clockwise direction to extract it. Burn the tick or drop it into alcohol. Clean the wound and apply an antiseptic ointment.

Ticks like to hide in the dog's ears and around the head, neck and anus. In tick season, check your dog regularly. Again, to break the life cycle, the immediate environment must also be treated by a professional exterminator.

If you live in an area where deer ticks are common, you will have to be extra cautious. They are very tiny and difficult to find. It is probably a good idea to get an annual vaccination that prevents Lyme disease in dogs. If your dog has not been vaccinated, you should be aware of the symptoms of Lyme disease. Lethargy, lameness, swollen joints and fever are the most obvious. Report these to your veterinarian as soon as you notice them.

Mites

These are tiny parasitic arachnids; that is, they are members of the spider family. Some cause demodectic mange, which causes hair loss with red, scaly patches. It is easily cured if it is not ignored. Sarcoptic mange also involves a mite. The symptoms are itching, loss of hair and skin encrustation. Secondary bacterial infections are common in both types of mange. The important thing here is early, vigorous veterinary treatment.

Ear mites can be the cause of dark, crumbly exudates in the ear. It is therefore wise to check all ear problems for the presence of mites as well as for yeast infections.

Worms

The other common kinds of parasites your dog is likely to encounter are internal worms. The most frequently observed species are roundworms, hookworms, whipworms, tapeworms and heartworms. All can be treated and eliminated with proper medications. It is important to have your veterinarian diagnose exactly what kind of parasite is present. The symptoms of parasitic infection are similar no matter which nasty creature is present.

These include general lethargy, appetite loss, diarrhea and blood in the stool. Weight loss, anemia and coat problems can be the result of severe infestations.

Your Wheaten should have an annual blood test for heartworm, which is transmitted by infected mosquitoes. There is a preventive medication available which your veterinarian will most likely prescribe. Over the counter preparations should not be used unless your vet recommends them.

This discussion of the various parasites that can affect your dog's health is included here to help make you a more informed Wheaten owner. This is even more true of the more serious disorders. This book is not meant to be a medical text, but rather to present some guidelines to help you know when to contact your veterinarian.

KIDNEY PROBLEMS IN THE WHEATEN

In recent years, serious kidney problems have been identified in Soft Coated Wheaten Terriers. Two are described as protein losing diseases—protein losing enteropathy (PLE) and protein losing nephropathy (PLN). The first involves the intestines and the second the kidneys. A protocol for screening has been developed by Dr. Meryl P. Littman at the University of Pennsylvania and Dr. Shelly Vaden at North Carolina State University Veterinary Schools. The symptoms for both conditions are similar. The symptoms of PLN are listlessness, depression, decreased appetite, vomiting,

weight loss, ascites (accumulation of fluid in the abdomen), edema and increased water consumption. PLE involves inflammatory bowel disease. In affected Wheatens there is stimulation of the immune system in the bowel wall. The usual symptoms are vomiting, diarrhea, weight loss, ascites, edema and pleural effusion.

At this point in time there is no conclusive evidence that PLE and PLN are inherited. However, because of the small gene pool within the breed, there is the possibility of a familial component. If the diseases are inherited, the mode of inheritance is complex. There also appears to be some relationship to diet and environmental stress. The SCWTCA is supporting research in the United States and Canada. Regular updated health committee reports are available from the SCWTCA. A screening protocol and post mortem protocol are also available. (See Appendix D.)

Another kidney condition that has been observed in Wheatens is renal dysplasia, in which the kidneys are malformed. In cases of RD, dogs usually die as youngsters. Renal dysplasia is thought to be inherited as a simple recessive gene, meaning both sire and dam carry the gene. Animals who produce RD should be removed from the gene pool as soon as their carrier status becomes known.

The preceding discussion has touched on treatable health problems as well as the more serious kidney problems in Wheatens. Again, this book is not a medical text. The material included here is meant to help Wheaten owners recognize problems and seek proper treatment.

CHAPTER 7

Caring for the Soft Coated Wheaten Terrier

Providing for your dog's basic needs is a vital part of the relationship between you and your Wheaten. He must be fed, exercised, trained and groomed. Training and grooming are discussed in Chapter 8 and Chapter 10. This chapter will deal primarily with exercise and diet.

EXERCISE

Soft Coated Wheaten Terriers are lively, exuberant animals. Just like people, they need sufficient exercise in order to maintain optimal good health. How much exercise does your Wheaten need? As much as he can get. To a great extent, it depends on his environment. If he has a safe fenced yard, he can run free and play to his heart's content. He can also express his terrier instinct to go to ground in your flower beds (if you let him). You may wish to fence in a smaller area where he can run without pulling up the pansies or pillaging the peonies. Smooth, round gravel is a good surface for a dog run; it will be easy to clean and will help keep the dog's feet in good condition. The enclosure should be long and fairly narrow so that he runs up and down rather than in circles. Probably a minimum dimension should be four feet by fifteen feet. A run should also be picked up and hosed at least once daily and be disinfected weekly especially in warmer weather or southern climates.

Any fencing should be high enough to keep him from jumping over. In my experience I have found that while Wheatens jump, most will respect the physical boundary a fence provides. However, you may have an escape artist who will climb or jump a fence. It is important to observe your dog's behavior to judge whether he might pull a "Houdini" on you. Never leave your dog in his run or yard unless you are home. Check often to see that all is well, especially when he is under a year old.

The best collar for a Wheaten is made of rolled leather. Keep your Wheaten's identification tags on the collar at all times. Tags may be obtained at local pet supply stores or by mail order. If you ship your dog by plane for any reason, use some sort of tape to fasten the dangling ID, rabies and license tags to the collar to prevent their getting caught in the wire openings of the crate door. Airlines require an attached water dish. Use a clip-on metal one, as stress may cause your dog to chew on the plastic ones the airlines provide. The small metal pans are inexpensive and can be lifesavers.

Some breeders have electronic chips inserted into their puppies before sending them to their new homes. The chip numbers must be registered with the provider and with AKC. Many lost dogs have been reclaimed through this method.

You may also have your dog tattooed. Most frequently, the owner's social security number or the dog's AKC registration number is used for this purpose. Some tattoos fade with time and may have to be done again. Be aware that there is no standard method and no requirements for people who do tattooing. If you elect to have your dog tattooed, make sure to find a reputable practitioner.

Proper identification will certainly make it easier for a lost dog to be reunited with his owner. However, vigilance on the owner's part is of the utmost importance. That sinking feeling that you get when you can't find your dog is truly frightening. As stated above, whenever your dog is in your safely fenced yard, check on him often.

If you live in an area where you cannot install a run or fencing, you might investigate invisible fencing. Many people have used it successfully. Invisible fencing involves buried wiring around the perimeter you choose. The dog wears a collar that emits an electronic pulse when it crosses the wire. This system is ineffective unless accompanied by proper conditioning and training and does not prevent other dogs from entering the area covered. This is not a do-it-yourself project. You will need to have the installer instruct you and help train your dog in order for the system to work properly.

Your new puppy will probably be happy with fifteen to thirty minutes of active play before needing a rest. As your puppy grows, it will need more structured activity. This means a long walk with his owner. A brisk half-hour walk twice a day will do a great deal of good. If you jog, put your dog on his leash and take him along. Make sure you introduce your dog to any fitness activity gradually.

Regular exercise is vital for any dog who spends a lot of time alone. Wheatens are people dogs. If they don't get enough time with their owner, they get bored and chew on the furniture or on themselves. Dogs need some kind of work too. This is where obedience training is useful. Teach your dog some tricks; countless behavior problems can be prevented by giving your dog sufficient exercise and human companionship.

TOYS

In addition to exercise, your dog should have the right toys to play with. Never give your Wheaten rawhide chews, pig ears or cow hooves; they gum up the Wheaten's coat as he chews and can cause intestinal blockage. Never play tug-of-war with your dog. Check the dog supply catalogs for hard nylon bones, hard latex balls and braided string toys. When your Wheaten is teething he will chew on almost anything.

The teething stage lasts from three to six months of age. The puppy will lose his "milk" teeth as the permanent teeth come in. Check the puppy's mouth frequently for double canines. These are the unshed canines from the milk teeth that remain alongside erupting permanent canines. If this occurs, contact your breeder or veterinarian. The baby canines should be removed in order to preserve the proper bite.

At this time the Wheaten's ear may also start to "fly" (assume unusual, usually undesirable positions). Again, check with your breeder to see about

Puppies love a good game of tug-of-war, but it should never be played between a dog and a person. Tug-of-war between you and your puppy has the potential to adversely affect his bite. (photo by Sally Sotirovich)

pasting the ears until the cartilage "sets." The SCWTCA *Owner's Manual* also discusses flying ears. If you have bought a show potential puppy, you will definitely want to set the ears, but doing so does not always work.

DIET AND NUTRITION

Dogs must eat to produce the energy needed to support all life functions. A properly balanced diet should contain enough fat, protein and carbohydrates to fulfill all of the dog's energy needs. These needs change throughout the dog's life. For example, a pregnant bitch must be fed differently from a growing puppy or an older dog. Basically, a dog must have sufficient nourishment to make the energy he needs to maintain his 101.5° body temperature. Any excess energy is used for all the dog's other activities (for example work, play, growth or convalescing among others).

Proteins, fat and carbohydrates are the main nutrients. Fat produces about twice the amount of energy as the other two. Thus if a diet is low in fat, the other nutrients will be used to maintain basal metabolism rather than for growth, enzyme production and other vital functions. Obviously, this is an inefficient way to feed.

In addition to protein, fat and carbohydrates, a dog needs vitamins, minerals and water, the last being the most vital. Water helps maintain body temperature, aids in digestion, produces energy and carries the other nutrients and enzymes to the dog's cells. Without adequate water, other functions cease and the dog dies.

Protein is made up of amino acids. A dog has a minimum daily requirement (MDR) for these building blocks of life. Some are made by the dog's cells but most come from the food the dog eats.

As stated earlier, fats are energy sources. They provide the means by which other nutrients enhance growth and activity. Dogs cannot manufacture essential fatty acids. In my experience, the addition of some fat or oil to a Wheaten's diet appears to be helpful in maintaining healthy skin and coat. Dogs store excess fat. Some excess fat is useful but if the dog gets too much he will keep storing it and become obese. A dog only becomes too fat from consuming more calories than he uses.

Carbohydrates also furnish energy. If the dog's diet is deficient in carbohydrates, the more valuable proteins will be used to produce glucose rather than being used for their more important work as building blocks of the cells.

Vitamins and minerals are the catalysts or triggers that help other chemical processes to occur. Minerals are particularly important because of their effects on other nutrients.

Wheatens, contrary to some opinions, are not picky eaters. Their owners make them that way when they try to make a food more enticing by adding table scraps to it. A Wheaten, or any dog for that matter, quickly learns that if he doesn't eat every bite as soon as his plate is offered, the owner, if so inclined, adds something to it. It is up to the owner to decide what to feed his pet. If the dog doesn't eat what is offered within ten or fifteen minutes, remove the plate and don't feed your dog until his next mealtime. Repeat this until he learns that if he does not eat when you decide to feed him, he won't eat at all. No normally healthy dog will starve himself.

Dogs do not need variety in their diet. They are creatures of habit and will happily and healthfully exist on the same food day after day, provided it is nutritionally adequate.

When choosing a dog food, read the label. By law, ingredients must be listed in descending order according to how much of each is contained in the can or bag. Select a dry food that has at least 7 percent fat, not less than 3 percent calcium, animal protein as one of the first four ingredients and at least one cereal grain. For canned foods, there should be at least 3 percent fats, less than 78 percent water and not less than 3 percent calcium and animal protein as one of the first two ingredients.

Semi-moist foods tend to have a lot of sugar and few Wheaten owners that I know use them. In my opinion, they are formulated to appeal to the owner rather than properly nourish the dog.

Although canned food is not recommended as a dog's only food, it can be added to kibble to moisten it and add that little extra taste. I prefer using boiled chopped beef or ground turkey as a flavoring. With the current emphasis on natural and organic foods, adding fresh meat has much to recommend it. The cost differential, if any, is negligible and the nutrition is at least equal, if not better.

Once or twice a week, you may add a cooked egg to your dog's regular food. Eggs are a highly digestible source of protein. Liver is also an excellent food that can be added to the dog's diet. Too much may cause diarrhea, so feed it in small amounts. Cottage cheese and yogurt are excellent sources of calcium.

When you get your puppy, your breeder will advise you about feeding. Her advice will probably

Like dogs everywhere, Wheatens are den animals, which is why Wheatens will normally seek to be under chairs or tables. They readily accept their crates. (photo by Marcie Granick)

differ from other breeders and from what is suggested here. As you gain more experience, you will develop your own patterns for feeding. Be aware that you are feeding a dog, not a person, and that foods designed for dogs are best for your Wheaten and easiest for you.

If you have purchased your puppy from a reliable hobby breeder, you probably received detailed feeding instructions. Every breeder has her own ideas about what to feed her dogs. The diet she suggests has been arrived at through years of breeding experience, and she has confidence in it. But keep in mind that there are many right ways to feed a dog.

The pet food industry is a multi-million dollar industry. Most breeders agree that kibble should comprise the major part of a dog's diet. A dog fed on a high quality kibble is probably better nourished than are many people. These foods are nutritionally complete. Much money and research goes into formulating foods that provide what dogs need in a palatable and digestible form.

When you get your new puppy, he will probably be eating three times a day. Do not follow the manufacturer's suggested amounts of kibble printed on the bag. Remember, the manufacturer wants to sell more dog food. Feed a growing puppy two to two and a half cups of kibble, divided so that the morning and evening meals are a bit larger than the noontime feeding. You will be eliminating this meal eventually.

Here is a sample diet and feeding schedule for a puppy from eight weeks to six months of age:

Morning   Feed one-half to three-quarter cups of kibble formulated for puppies and softened with warm water. Add one-quarter of a cooked egg and one tablespoon of cottage cheese.

Owning multiple Wheatens can be a challenge, but if handled properly, it can be a rewarding experience. (photo by Sally Sotirovich)

Noon   Feed one-half cup softened kibble with a tablespoon of canned food formulated for puppies.

Evening   Feed one-half to three-quarter cup softened kibble, a tablespoon of canned puppy food and sprinkle in about a tablespoon of powdered milk.

By the time your dog is a year old, change to a food formulated for the adult dog. According to Dr. Donald Collins, author of *The Collins Guide to Dog Nutrition* (New York: Howell Book House, 1987), a forty-pound adult dog kept as a household pet needs 1,160 calories per day. A thirty-two-pound dog needs fewer than 1,000 calories per day. If you calculate your dog's diet based on these needs, obesity will not rear its ugly head for your Wheaten friend.

Most owners will probably feed an adult dog once a day. Others may wish to divide the food into a morning and evening meal. When to feed your full-grown Wheaten is a personal decision. Some professional handlers and breeders feed in the late evening, particularly if a show dog needs more weight. My present dog tends to be somewhat on the "chunky" side. I feed my dog in the morning so that she burns calories during the day. That seems to work for us.

Dogs get used to whatever routine their owners decide to follow. The important thing is to have a regular routine. Feed and walk the dog at about the same time each day. An adult dog needs to relieve himself at least three or four times a day. An older dog may need even more outings. Remember, no matter what the weather is, a dog has to be taken out to relieve himself. There can be some flexibility in your dog's schedule, but, in general, dogs feel more secure when they know what to expect from their owners and their environment.

Grooming the Soft Coated Wheaten Terrier

Any owner of a Soft Coated Wheaten Terrier can and should learn to perform the basic grooming needed to keep his dog clean and looking like a Wheaten. Ring presentation is admittedly more detailed and is discussed in Chapter 9.

Grooming can be a relaxing time of togetherness for owner and dog or a painful, tedious ordeal for either or both. It all depends on how much effort is put into the project. The fundamentals involve bathing, combing and brushing, nail cutting and coat trimming. Assuming your puppy has been obtained from a reliable hobby breeder, he should have some acquaintance with a grooming table, comb and brush, scissors and nail clippers. If not, you will have to provide this training as soon as possible.

EQUIPMENT

You will need to acquire some standard equipment to produce the desired results. The first item will be a grooming table. A folding model, made specifically for grooming dogs, can be purchased by mail order from dog equipment suppliers or at dog shows. The table is made to accommodate a chrome "grooming arm" fitted with a collar attachment to hold the dog still. The grooming arm is best described as an inverted "L" that attaches to the top of the table. If you prefer, it is also possible to improvise. Rubber matting can be permanently attached to or placed on any solid table or surface at a comfortable height for you and with secure footing for your Wheaten. You can buy a clamp-on grooming arm or hang a collar attachment from an overhead hook. However, a grooming table is one of the best investments a Wheaten owner can make. They are manufactured in several sizes. I use one that is eighteen inches by thirty inches, and I wouldn't be without it.

The table is important because the dog will associate it with grooming. Those who have tried to groom a dog on the floor soon learn that it is just useless. Once a dog becomes accustomed to being on the table, he will enjoy the attention and will stand or lie down as long as is necessary.

It helps to get the puppy used to the grooming process if you make initial sessions short and pleasurable. While a young puppy does not have much coat compared to the typical adult, brief periods of combing and brushing help accustom him to the sensation of being groomed. Schedule these grooming sessions several times a week when you first get your puppy.

Also, after your puppy has learned good "grooming manners" on the table and has developed complete confidence in you, teach him to lie on his side on the table. This training is very easy to do and makes grooming much easier on both you and your dog. To do this, grasp the puppy's front and rear leg on your far side and gently lay

This is not a recommended way to comb a Wheaten. (photo by Mary Lou Lafler)

the dog on the table. Your dog may struggle at first, but speak soothingly and encouragingly and soon he will probably relax. Now, with one hand on his ribs, gently brush his side coat. Praise the puppy lavishly when he holds the position and gradually increase the time span he is on his side. Eventually you will even be able to turn your dog on to his other side without his even getting up! When teaching a puppy to lie down for grooming, *never* perform any operation, such as cutting nails or combing out snarls, that might cause discomfort. Afterward, offer a treat while the puppy is on the table. Play with him and praise him for his good manners.

The Wheaten coat requires frequent combing and brushing. Steel combs with slightly rounded teeth are best. These combs are available at pet stores, dog shows and through dog supply catalogs. As a rule, dog show vendors feature the widest selection of combs and brushes and an inventory

The best way to clean this dog—short of a complete bath— is to let the mud dry and then brush it out. (photo by Sally Sotirovich)

Others choose combs with no handles at all. I prefer a seven-inch metal comb with no handle with half the teeth closer together and the other half farther apart, essentially combining a medium and a finer comb in one unit. Get a good comb as such a one will last indefinitely. Pinching pennies on grooming equipment is always a false economy.

A pin brush with good cushioning in the base does the best job on a Wheaten coat. These brushes resemble human wig brushes. Most have wooden handles, but some are of man-made materials. The important thing is that the pins not be too sharp. I once tried a brush with little ball-shaped protectors on the pins and found it ineffective. You may have to try several types to find the most suitable one for you.

A slicker brush has fine wire teeth. It can be used to remove the tiny fuzz balls after you have used the regular pin brush. The slicker takes out more coat than your pin brush, but it is a useful tool. The best slicker brushes have soft bristles slightly bent at the tips. They are easier on the coat than other models. The slicker is also helpful in separating mats or lifting the coat before trimming.

You will need three different kinds of scissors: blunt-nosed, straight and thinning shears. Blunt or round tipped scissors are used between the toes, on the inside of the ears, near the eyes, anus and genitals. The points are rounded but the blades are sharp. Straight scissors are used for trimming the feet and what I call *gross trimming*, that is, trimming the longest hairs in order to get the beginning of the terrier outline.

Thinning shears are scissors with teeth. In some models, both blades have teeth, while others

of special equipment that would be hard to find anywhere else. Ask your breeder where he or she shops for Wheaten supplies.

Select a comb that feels comfortable to you. Some people prefer a comb fitted with a wooden handle or a one-piece metal comb with handle.

Combination combs.

Pictured on this page are some of the grooming tools required for making the most of a Soft Coated Wheaten Terrier's appearance. What they are and how to use them are fully described in the text.

Straight barber's scissors.

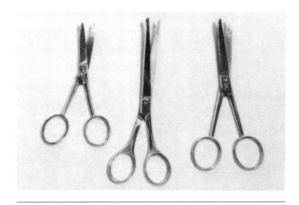

Blunt-nosed shears.

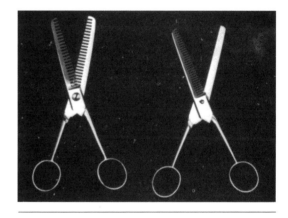

Double- and single-serrated thinning shears.

have one straight and one serrated blade. I use both kinds. The latter removes more coat at each cut. Thinning shears give a more uneven, natural look to the trimmed coat. They also thin by removing some of the hair on the spots where it grows thicker, such as the neck, thighs, shoulders and loins. The advantage of these is that they don't leave scissors marks. Again, buy good quality scissors and keep them clean, dry and sharp.

A mat splitter is a useful piece of equipment. It will break up a mat and enable you to comb it away. There are two basic types. I prefer the model with about a dozen sharp blades and a handle. The blades can be replaced when they become dull. This tool must be used sparingly as it does remove a great deal of coat. The other type has a curved handle and uses an injector-type razor blade. This

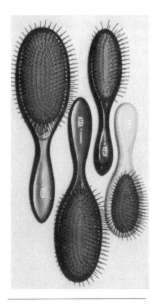

Pin brushes.

one requires a bit more skill, as it really takes out a lot of coat. The best plan is to groom your Wheaten often enough so that you never need a mat splitter to begin with.

Nail clippers of some kind are an absolute must. There is a type called a guillotine and another called a scissors type. An electric grinder with various attachments is also available. If you opt for automation, accustom the puppy to the noise and feel of the grinder at a very early age. Some dogs just will not accept it at all while others are more tolerant of a grinder than of a manual nail clipper. A three-sided file can be used for smoothing off the rough edges.

A hemostat (Kelly forceps) is not an absolute necessity, but it is handy for cleaning hair out of the ears and removing ticks. It can be used to hold a cotton ball or gauze for cleaning ears or applying medication. Cotton swabs and cotton balls serve a number of purposes and should also be part of your grooming kit.

COMBING AND BRUSHING

Now that you have all this equipment, where do you start? How do you use these unfamiliar implements? Let us begin with combing and brushing. First check for mats. The beard, the chest, the neck, under the front legs, the elbows, the loin area and inside the thighs are the places where matting most frequently occurs. When the coat is going through the changes from its puppy to adult texture, mats appear as if by magic. It is important to comb and brush almost daily during the interval of these changes, which can last from six months until the dog is two years old. A spray-on coat dressing helps control matting and makes combing easier.

To remove small mats, use the end of your comb in a slicing motion. When the mat is broken into ever smaller mats, you will be able to comb the hair right out from the skin or use the slicker. While you are working on the mat with one hand, hold the hair close to the skin with your other hand so that you are not pulling the coat and hurting the dog. Remember, grooming need never be a painful ordeal for you or your Wheaten.

For large mats, more drastic measures may be needed. This is when you use your mat splitter. If you are using a model with multiple blades, place it at the part of the mat nearest to the body. Drawing the mat splitter toward you, slowly slice through the mat while holding the coat so as to minimize pulling. Make one pass at a time, then comb. As the mat is broken into smaller parts, you can revert to your metal comb and proceed as previously described. Here again, a coat dressing will make the job considerably easier for you and the dog.

The curved mat splitter is used in a slightly different way, but the result is essentially the same; it makes the mat progressively smaller until it can be easily combed out. Hold the blade so that it enters the side of the mat and splits it in layers. Each layer can then be treated separately. If your dog gets burrs or gum in his coat you may have to cut the entire mat out with the possibility of leaving a "hole." Don't be dismayed. Remember, the coat will grow back.

Once the dog is free of mats, combing and brushing can begin. Start with the head combing the fall forward being careful near the eyes. Make a part down the nose and comb the hair straight down on either side of the muzzle. Next turn your attention to the beard. If it is greasy or contains food particles, rub a bit of cornstarch into the hair before combing.

Now proceed to the ears, neck and chest. This is where you use your brush. As you move down over the body, it may help to have the dog lie on his side as described earlier in this chapter. You can make yourself more comfortable if you sit on a high stool during at least part of the session. When you are working on the body, brush the coat from the skin out, working in layers. This removes the little "fuzz-balls" that will eventually form into mats. Be sure to get right down to the skin whenever you brush or comb your Wheaten.

When both sides are brushed, stand the dog and comb the coat thoroughly. While you are learning and practicing your grooming skills, you may wish to break the process into several sessions. It is important to make grooming pleasant for you and your dog. Never groom or train if you are tired and irritable. Take a break whenever you or your dog get restless.

Now that the head and body are combed and brushed, it is time for the feet and legs. These areas can be sensitive as there is not much flesh on them as compared to other parts of the body, so be as gentle as you can.

With the dog lying on his side, you can start on the outside of the legs closest to you and the insides of the legs that are furthest away. Then, simply turn the dog over and repeat the procedure on the other side. You can also cut the hair between the pads at this point. If your dog will not lie on the table, you will have to comb legs and feet with the dog standing. This is not as easy, but it can be done.

THE BATH

Different dogs react differently to bathing. Some dogs love it; others tolerate it and still others hate every minute. My older Wheaten would get into the tub even when the bath was being run for a human member of the household. Her daughter, on the other hand, howled through the whole process and had to be fastened by her collar in the tub.

Have a lot of towels and your shampoos and rinses handy. You can probably wash a young puppy in the kitchen sink or in a laundry tub. If this bothers your sensibilities, purchase some kind of tub that will hold an adult dog or use the family tub as most owners do. Make sure the tub has a non-slip surface. Some people even take the dog into their stall showers to get the job done.

Always use shampoo meant for dogs. Many products are tear-free and can be used on both the head and body. If you have a flea problem, use a medicated product. (Not on the head, please.) Some good ones are available from your veterinarian or pet supply houses.

The bath water should be moderately warm. Inserting cotton in the ears to keep water out is a wise precaution against avoidable ear problems. A hand spray is necessary for wetting the dog down and rinsing thoroughly. After the dog is wet, work the shampoo lather completely through the coat. Pay special attention to the rear and to the feet. Don't skip the belly. Rinse thoroughly with the hand spray.

After the shampoo has been thoroughly removed, a creme rinse or detangling product should be used. Some of these must be rinsed out and others are left in. Follow the manufacturer's directions and, if rinsing is called for, do it thoroughly.

When the bath is over, pat your dog with towels until the excess water is absorbed. You can continue to use towels or put the dog on the grooming table and use a hair dryer (on low or medium setting) to hasten the process, brushing at the same time. With my present Wheaten, I prefer to let her dry naturally unless it is really cold so that the natural wave is not straightened by blow-drying.

A Wheaten's nails are rather hard. Cutting them right after a bath is somewhat easier than doing so when they are dry. In any event, they should be shortened weekly. See the section on nails under "Routine Maintenance" and the diagrams for instructions in Chapter 6.

When the dog is dry, you can begin combing and brushing the coat. Since your dog was thoroughly combed, brushed and de-matted before his bath, it should be relatively easy to do this brushing. With the dog lying on his side, back brush layer by layer, moving the brush from the skin outward to the ends of the hair. With the dog standing, back brush from tail to head. Brush the fall forward and the muzzle coat down on each side. Brush front and rear leg hair up. When the entire coat has been brushed, finish by combing the entire dog with the lay of the coat. Now your dog is ready to trim. However, let him rest before you commence; he deserves it.

TRIMMING

Trimming is a skill that will improve with practice. If you are not planning to show your dog, you can trim as much or as little as you care to do. However, always remember, the impression your Wheaten makes on the public reflects on the breed as a whole and on your care in particular. A shorn Wheaten is not attractive.

Even if you want to keep your dog's coat in a completely natural state, trimming must be done between the pads, around the feet, the anus, genitals and the ears. Too much hair on the ears prevents air circulation and can lead to infections. An overly long beard means water is dripped on the floor when the dog drinks. Food can stick to the hair and

An ungroomed Wheaten on a grooming table, which is considered required equipment for any Wheaten owner.

The Standard calls for a dog who looks "square" in outline. Keep this in mind when you are trimming. Having a picture of a well-trimmed Wheaten to refer to is helpful, as is SCWTCA's grooming chart.

With the dog standing, using thinning shears, trim down the front from the neck over the chest and down the legs. Don't shorten too much at this stage. Next, set the line of the rear by trimming fairly close behind the tail, over the rear and down to the hocks. Using the blunt-nosed scissors, clean hair short around the anus and genitals. Clean out the longer hair on the inside of the hind legs.

Now fluff comb the back coat from the shoulders to the base of the tail. Shorten the coat along the back to achieve a level topline. Shorten and blend the hair at the front and along the sides of the tail. As a hint, from the rear the tail should look like a little Christmas tree.

After the topline is completed, move down the sides blending the coat by trimming and thinning. Be sure to leave enough length to flow when the dog moves.

Now we go back to the head. Remove the fringe along the edges of the ears. Hold the ear so that you can feel where flesh ends and hair begins. Clean all hair from the underside of the ear using blunt-nosed scissors. Check the ear canal for signs of infection and for excess hair in the canal itself. Gently remove the hair with your fingers or a

cause odor. There is a certain amount of trimming that should be a part of your dog's basic hygiene. Your Wheaten deserves to be kept clean and neat, the demands of the show ring notwithstanding.

Now you are ready to begin trimming. Stand your clean, combed-out dog on the table. Observe him from all angles and decide which areas need to be trimmed to achieve the outline you want. Placing your grooming table in front of a large mirror is most helpful in checking your progress.

The same dog after bathing and grooming.

longer at the crease so that it blends into the head coat.

In trimming the head, the idea is to achieve a rectangular look from both the top and the sides. This is done by cutting the topknot fairly short between the ears to about one and a half inches. Proceed toward the eyes, leaving the hair longer as you proceed to create the fall. The fall should not go beyond the nose. If you lift the fall and trim the area immediately over the eyes quite short, it forms a shelf that supports the longer hair and enables the dog to see better without exposing his eyes. You may also thin the hair directly over the eyes to create a veil effect without exposing the eyes.

Proceed slowly at first, taking only one or two cuts before combing the cut hair out. Never forget that the hair will grow back and any mistakes you make will be erased naturally.

Thin the cheek area next. Cut and comb through. Do this gradually so that you do not remove too much coat. You want the cheeks to look flat, so it is necessary to thin the areas where the coat grows thick. You want to avoid a lumpy look. Again, look at the head from all sides and trim the beard so that the look is balanced and rectangular.

The throat, neck and chest areas will characteristically have dense coat. These areas mat easily and are sensitive to pulling and tugging. These sections may now be thinned and tipped relatively short but

Kelly forceps (hemostat). Using medicated ear powder makes the job easier by soothing the ear canals and a little on your fingertips improves your grip.

Cut away the hair from the area just below the canal to allow air circulation. Trim the outer surface of the ear with the thinning shears. Back comb and trim with the scissors pointing up from the point of the ear. This will make it easier to blend the hair and achieve a smooth look without taking off too much coat. The ear coat should be should never appear shaved. Care should be taken to blend the coat gradually down the neck into the shoulders and topline and into the front legs.

On the front legs the goal is to create columns. Again, fluff combing is the desired technique. Hair can be completely removed from the "arm pit" area, as matting frequently occurs here. The inside of the elbow will probably need thinning. If the coat on the legs is too long, its weight causes it to hang.

Looking at your Wheaten from the side, begin creating a curving line with the lowest point at the elbow and the highest at the loin with a final blending into the rear leg. Comb and tip the coat. Try to make both sides match. This is where the mirror is helpful.

You can clean the hair off the center of the belly and leave the side coat to act as a curtain. This is a particularly good idea for males, as it cuts down on odor from urine hitting the hair on the abdomen. You can create the illusion of a dog with longer or shorter legs, depending upon how much coat you remove.

The rear legs are thinned and tipped using "fluff" combing. This means using your comb to lift the coat away from the leg with a flip. You can then tip the hairs that stand outside your imaginary lines. The idea is to give a straight line from hip to ground. If you notice any bumpy areas, thin them so the line is smooth.

Coat tends to grow down over the rump and creates what looks like a skirt when viewed from the rear. Tip and blend carefully to achieve a smooth line. Tip and thin the hock area so that it is

cylindrical from all angles. Be sure to leave enough coat on the lower legs to balance with the front legs.

Finally, we get to the feet. With the dog standing, use your straight scissors. Keeping them almost parallel to the table, trim the coat to create a rounded foot. Nails should not visibly protrude from under the coat. The foot should be trimmed to complete the column.

Now stand back and look at your handiwork. If it's less than perfect, don't be discouraged. It takes time to become an expert, and the coat will grow back again.

This section on grooming is designed to help the new Wheaten owner to learn the basic procedures essential for properly grooming these dogs. While it is not nearly as detailed as it could be, it does enable the new owner to keep a Soft Coated Wheaten Terrier presentable. Additional directions concerning ring presentation are given in Chapter 9, which covers showing your dog.

The official grooming chart, the SCWTCA *Owners' Manual* and the *Illustrated Standard* can be purchased directly from the Soft Coated Wheaten Terrier Club of America. (If you decide to have your local groomer trim your dog, purchase a copy for her or him, too.) The AKC will provide the current address of the Club's secretary. All three publications should be part of your dog library.

POINTS TO REMEMBER

Everyone who owns one or more Soft Coated Wheaten Terrier, or who is attracted to the breed and decides to add a Wheaten to the household, must remember the breed's absolute need for regular, systematic grooming. Any deep-coated dog needs regular attention to his coat. The Wheaten whose coat is neglected is a prime target for the ravages of external parasites, undetected skin conditions, tumors and related health problems. In addition, without regular grooming, the Wheaten will be deprived of important personal interaction and quality time with a caring owner. Grooming, then, should not be looked upon as a tedious chore, but rather as an opportunity to create a bond between dog and owner that really makes for a priceless relationship.

Your introduction to the Wheaten probably came about as a result of seeing a photo in a book or magazine or a live dog on the street or at a dog show. Perhaps you saw a Wheaten on television and that was the spark that drew you to the breed. There is every chance that the Wheaten that started it all for you was clean and well groomed. Just remember that the breed just doesn't grow that way and getting that look takes work.

You now know from reading this chapter and the next that you can make the most of your Wheaten. You know what to do and where to get additional help. Doing it is all up to you. Your Wheaten can reflect beauty and good care or sad neglect. Either way, your dog's condition speaks volumes about you as a fully committed dog owner. Like a well-kept car and beautiful clothes, a well-trained, well-groomed dog is a thing of beauty and a source of personal pride. Remember the place of good grooming in your Wheaten's life and you will always be able to take justifiable pride in his appearance.

(photo © Marcie Grannick)

Given the opportunity, the resourceful Wheaten can always arrange for his own creature comforts. (photo by Jane Elkin Thomas)

A Soft Coated Wheaten Terrier knows how to relax and enjoy life. (photo by Diane Fleming)

This eye-catching threesome consists of (from left) Krissie, K.C. and Golda, owned by Betsy Geertson, and all have made their mark in competitive Obedience.

"Is this what I'm supposed to do?" seems to be the question posed by this inquisitive youngster owned and bred by Sylvia and Bill Hamilton. (photo by Lori-Anne McDermid)

Herding comes naturally to the Soft Coated Wheaten Terrier. It was just one of the many tasks assigned to Wheatens on the Irish farms where they developed. (photo by J. Price)

"Wheaten in the willows." (photo by John Ashbey)

The Wheaten, a dog of many talents. Here Betsy Geertson follows behind an intense Tracking dog.

Am., Can. Ch. Desertsun's Chermar, CD, taking a demanding jump during an Agility Trial. (photo by Robert Bloom)

Wheatens tend to age gracefully, remaining youthful far into their senior years. (photo by Close Encounters of the Furry Kind)

"How much longer do we have to sit here?"
(photo by Dana Frady)

Ch. Raclee Express West O'Andover, CD, ROM, bred by Ruth Stein and owned by Cindy Vogels, was Best of Breed at the national Specialty in 1975 and the first Roving Specialty in 1976. (photo by G. Gottlieb)

Dog shows provide recreation for all fanciers and afford the public a prime opportunity to see and learn about the breeds. This group of Wheaten exhibitors and their dogs wait patiently for their chance to show the judge what they've got. (photo by Bill West)

It's at the Specialties that the clubs and the entire fancy put a collective "best foot forward." As most national terrier clubs, the SCWTCA holds its principal Specialty with the Montgomery County KC show in Ambler, Pennsylvania, in early October. In this presentation to Ch. Hilltop's Ain't Misbehavin', the color and beauty of this classic event are just two of its unforgettable aspects. Imagine a show with some 200 Wheatens entered. Attend once, and you will always want to return. (photo by John Ashbey)

Tea for two. (photo by Mary Lou Lafler)

Wheatens have a definite rapport with autumn leaves. (photo by Marcie Granick)

Your Wheaten will joyfully join you for anything you may wish to do. (photo by Sandy Newfield)

Like all the dogs of Ireland, the Soft Coated Wheaten Terrier has a natural affinity for the water—whether on a boat in its midst or contemplating it from the shore. To share that affinity with his own special person is truly Wheaten heaven. (photo by Sydney Fisher)

(photo by Mary Lou Lafler)

CHAPTER 9

Showing Your
Soft Coated Wheaten Terrier

ABOUT DOG SHOWS

Organized dog shows began in England during the last half of the 19th century. The American Kennel Club was formed by a group of sportsmen in Philadelphia, Pennsylvania, in 1884 to administer dog shows and field trials. Later it started its Stud Book register that recorded dogs' names together with those of their sires and dams.

A dog show provides an opportunity for breeders to exhibit their stock in competition with other breeders. It is a good idea to attend a few dog shows to see whether the idea of participating appeals to you. One thing to remember is that in a dog show there are always more losers than winners. This is no place for the overly sensitive. Talk to exhibitors and handlers to get a feel for the game. After doing so, remember to be objective and make your own choices about becoming a participant.

Showing Your Dog

One of the most personally rewarding experiences you can have is to show your Wheaten to his championship. If you have purchased an animal with show potential, take the time to learn about showing your own dog. If you have the temperament for it, find a dog handling class in your area where you can develop your skills. These are usually run by dog clubs and many good books on the subject are also available. As you spend time grooming and training, you and your dog will develop a special relationship. When you show, you will meet other Wheaten owners and expand your circle of friends.

Showing is not difficult, but it does require some preparation. In a show, the dog has to walk around a ring on a lead, tail up, in a pattern indicated by the judge. For the novice, this may seem to be a daunting proposition, but getting that championship certificate is well worth it. If you would rather have someone else show your dog, you can hire a professional handler. This is usually a highly-skilled person who will take your dog and prepare it completely for competition. The handler charges a fee for showing your dog as well as his board and any bonuses that may apply to special wins. Most handlers also prorate their travel expenses among all clients on the same show trip. Obviously, it is wise to review the handler's rate card and discuss your goals before turning over your dog. Financial arrangements vary with the individual handler, so be sure you know in advance what you are paying for.

If you do take this route, be sure you have confidence in the person. Ask for references and check him or her out. There are organizations such as the Professional Handlers' Association and the Dog Handler's Guild whose members follow specific guidelines regarding their conduct. The AKC can help you locate the current secretaries. Remember, this person will be responsible for your dog's care and feeding for as long as it takes to get the title or you decide to stop showing. Learn as much as you can about him or her and their facilities.

Before you start exhibiting in formal championship (point) shows, you should enter your dog in match shows. These are more casual events where dogs, judges and exhibitors all participate to gain experience. No points are awarded. Puppies younger than six months may be entered. Entry fees are substantially lower than at point shows. Since every AKC all-breed club has to conduct one match each year, there are plenty of opportunities for practice.

If your goal is to "finish" your dog, (win a championship title), the more experience you and your dog have, the better your chances are of acquiring the points you will need. If you prepare yourself and your dog in advance, when you go into that ring you will be comfortable and relaxed and so will your dog. This is a place where showmanship and condition matter *very* much.

Dogs competing in point shows are always pre-entered. The AKC can provide you with the official entry forms on request. After you have entered one or two shows, you will automatically receive

❏ MASTER or ❏ VISA   FOR FAX ENTRY ONLY - FEE $4 PER ENTRY   EXPIRATION DATE
CARD NO.

CARD HOLDER
NAME

SHOW | DATE

I ENCLOSE $_____ for entry fees.
IMPORTANT - Read Carefully Instructions on Reverse Side Before Filling Out. Numbers in the boxes
indicate sections of the instructions relevant to the information needed in that box. (PLEASE PRINT)

BREED	VARIETY (1)	SEX

DOG (2) (3) SHOW CLASS		CLASS (3) DIVISION Weight, Color, etc.
ADDITIONAL CLASSES	OBEDIENCE TRIAL CLASS	JR. SHOWMANSHIP CLASS

NAME OF (See Back)
JUNIOR HANDLER (if any)

FULL NAME
OF
DOG

❏ AKC REG. NO.   Enter number here | DATE OF BIRTH
❏ AKC LITTER NO.
❏ ILP NO. | PLACE OF   ❏ USA   ❏ CANADA   ❏ FOREIGN
❏ FOREIGN REG NO. & COUNTRY | BIRTH   Do not print the above in catalog

BREEDER

SIRE

DAM

ACTUAL
OWNER(S)_____   Please Check If
(4)   (Please Print)   ❏ OWNERSHIP CHANGE
OWNER'S
ADDRESS   ❏ ADDRESS CHANGE

CITY _____ STATE _____ ZIP _____
NAME OF OWNER'S AGENT
(IF ANY) AT THE SHOW _____ ID # _____

I CERTIFY that I am the actual owner of the dog, or that I am the duly authorized agent of the actual owner whose name I have entered
above. In consideration of the acceptance of this entry, I (we) agree to abide by the rules and regulations of The American Kennel Club
in effect at the time of this show or obedience trial, and by any additional rules and regulations appearing in the premium list for this
show or obedience trial or both, and further agree to be bound by the Agreement printed on the reverse side of this entry form. I (we)
certify and represent that the dog entered is not a hazard to persons or other dogs. This entry is submitted for acceptance on the
foregoing representation and agreement.

SIGNATURE of owner or his agent
duly authorized to make this entry _____

Telephone _____ Pers. ID Code # _____

Sample entry form used for all AKC conformation shows and obedience trials.

premium lists (announcements) of upcoming shows from the superintendents covering the shows in your area. Subscribing to the *AKC Gazette* will bring you a calendar of events each month along with the magazine.

To become an AKC champion, a dog must earn fifteen points under at least three different judges. Two of the wins must be of three, four or five points or "major" wins and they may not be made under the same judge. Points are determined by the number of dogs defeated and the geographical area in which the show is held. The schedule is reviewed annually and adjusted up or down as the situation warrants.

A dog is entered in one of six classes; Puppy, Twelve to Eighteen months, Novice, American Bred, Bred by Exhibitor and Open. At some shows, puppy classes may be divided by age with one class for puppies over six and under nine months of age and a second for puppies over nine months and under a year.

The winners of each class compete against each other for the judge to select Winners Dog and Winners Bitch. These dogs are awarded the points and can continue to compete with the champions entered for Best of Breed competition. Champions are often called "specials"—a holdover term from before the mid-1960s.

Within breed competition, Best of Breed is the top award. The BOB dog is eligible to compete in Group competition. After designating his BOB, the judge will also select a Best of Winners (BOW) and a Best of Opposite Sex (BOS) to the Best of Breed dog in that order. The Best of Winners dog

or bitch is awarded the higher number of points (if applicable) available in either sex. If a class dog goes BOB or BOS and defeats champions in the process, additional points can be won. However, no more than five points can be won at any show regardless of the award or the size of the entry.

A young prospect, groomed and ready to enter the ring. (photo by Jeff Dorl)

RING PRESENTATION

Another significant aspect of showing a Soft Coated Wheaten Terrier is ring presentation. Proper presentation goes well beyond the basic everyday grooming and trimming discussed in Chapter 8. The following section on ring presentation was written by Marjorie Shoemaker, a longtime breeder

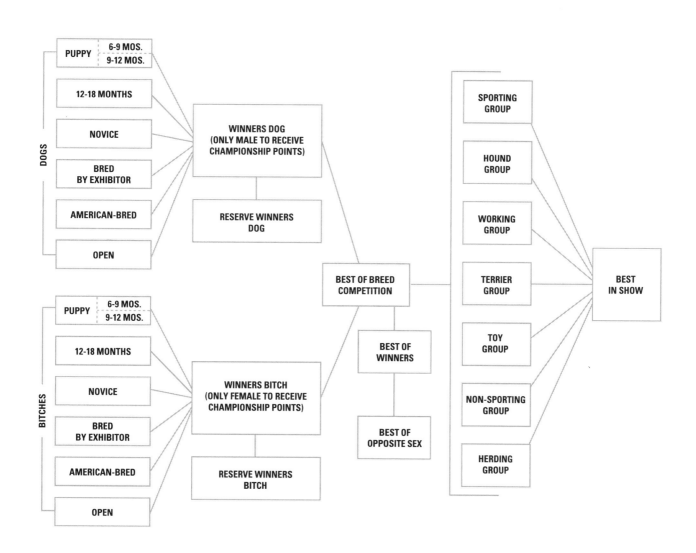

A group of exhibitors in a relaxed moment in the ring. These dogs have been examined and are waiting for the judge to finish with their class. (photo by Bill West)

and exhibitor. I am most grateful for her help. Follow her lead, groom your dog, go for that title and have fun!

The Soft Coated Wheaten Terrier is a challenge to trim for show presentation. The breed Standard uses the word "natural" in reference to the dog's appearance and grooming. Perhaps the term "naturalize" would be more appropriate. The coat should be left long enough to retain this more natural look, yet be tidy enough to maintain a terrier outline in motion or at those windy outdoor shows.

The Wheaten should never appear ragged, bunchy-coated or heavy-coated, the result of under-trimming or over-tipping. When the dog is moving, this unevenness of coat is a distraction. Clumps of hair flopping in odd places or straggling where they should flow obstruct the appearance of good terrier outline and movement.

The look to be shunned is the clipped or tipped look where all the hair is shortened evenly to a terrier outline. The effect is that of a Bichon Frise or a Kerry Blue trim. This is incorrect and should be penalized in the ring although it is often seen. This "sculpted" puffy look is NOT natural. The effect should be one of easy laying of hair into gentle waves. The coat should waft (or flow) as the dog moves rather than bounce and pop.

The rule of thumb is to make the Wheaten appear to be NATURALLY stylish; NEVER should it appear unnaturally stylized. There should be NO evidence of scissoring.

Basic Rules

1. Have a picture of the ideal in your mind, and use the hair to create this image.

2. Consider the dog as three dimensional; the hair is your medium. Move around the dog and view areas from all angles as you work.

3. NEVER trim a dirty or matted dog.

4. Work slowly at first, taking time to put the dog on the floor to check your work as the dog moves.

5. Finalize your work by having someone stack and gait the dog; remove all the floppies, bunchies and whispies you see.

Tools

• *Thinning shears*—They are hereafter referred to as shears, to differentiate them from straight-bladed scissors. These will be your most valuable tool; these shears are what creates the more natural look by using thinning and tipping. Economy™ single-edged shears are a recommended brand.

• *Straight-edged scissors*—These scissors are used mainly to trim ear outlines, feet and of course, for low-maintenance pet trims.

• *Comb*— The Greyhound™ comb is a metal comb with narrow tines or teeth that can penetrate a thick Wheaten coat to the skin. There are several models of this comb that vary in length and some have medium- and wide-spaced tines in the same comb. This is a very important tool.

• *Pin brush*—This is usually an oval-shaped brush with a rubber cushion in which pins are imbedded. It is used for blow-drying and brushing out the coat.

• *Slicker brush*—This brush is rectangular in shape and has a rubber cushion in which fine bent pins are imbedded. It is used for de-matting and separating coat.

• *Electric clipper* (optional)—This can be used on the underside of the ear leathers, between the pads of the feet and for cleaning off the stomach area. Its use requires some skill.

Terminology

• *Tipping*—This process removes the length of the coat. Tipping also reduces a coat's weight and causes shortened areas to stand out or up, like a crew-cut.

• *Thinning*—This process removes the thickness of the coat. This process will allow the weight of coat that is left to lay better.

• *Back-combing* (or fluff-combing)—This is the process of combing an area of the coat backwards or out from the body to check the overall appearance and length of an area.

• *Blending*—This is the process of graduating coat length and density from the closely trimmed areas around the underside of the neck and the rear to the longer coated areas along the sides and topline. This technique is a vital part of creating the more natural look. It is a combination of tipping and thinning around the corners of the dog.

• *Popping*—This is the effect created by the coat standing out from the body. This occurs when a dog moves, and is very evident if the dog is over-tipped.

Key Points

To recap what has already been given, the major factors in properly grooming a Wheaten are:

1. Have a strong mental image of your finished product. Your image should include covering or minimizing your dog's faults while enhancing his virtues. Use a photograph of a well-trimmed Wheaten if you have problems picturing the dog in your mind. Author's note: Consult the *Illustrated Standard* for guidance.

2. Use thinning shears to create a natural look and to avoid any appearance of scissoring.

3. Blend the short areas to the longer coat using the thinning/tipping combination.

4. NEVER cut across the hair; always use the shears following the direction in which the coat lies.

It cannot be emphasized enough that the proper way to groom a Wheaten is to "naturalize" the trimming by use of the thinning shears in the tipping/thinning combination. This is time consuming but in the end, rewarding.

THE OVERALL OUTLINE

The first step is to stand at the side of the dog and "block out" his outline, by working on the forequarters and then the rear. The area under the jaw at the junction of the head and neck and down the front of the chest to the beginning of the legs should be trimmed fairly short. The rear profile from the tail down the rear leg and the slope to the hock should be trimmed rather closely as well. I use thinning shears for all of this unless the dog

Wheaten in the rough.

Setting up the outline.

has not been groomed for a long time, in which case I would use straight blades, staying at least one half inch from the skin.

I return to the thinning shears to do the more precise trimming. After cleaning off both ends of the dog, step back and look at the effect. Decide where you want to locate the height of the topline to balance the dog's length with his height. Take into account the length of the dog's neck and his legs. Set the topline in with your shears.

Now the outline has been roughly set in. Proceed to work with your shears from the underside of the neck along the side of the neck and down to the shoulder. Tip these areas first, following the lay of the coat with your shears, not cutting across the coat. Thin the thick, bunchy areas by inserting the tips of the shears into the coat and next to the skin (again in the direction the coat lays, not across the coat).

Some people might prefer using double-edged shears to thin because they can use a larger blade surface than just the tips of the single edged shears. I have found that I alternate thinning and tipping techniques so often, that it would be a waste of time to change from one type of shears to another.

COMPLETE ONE SIDE AT A TIME

It has been my experience that it is better to work on one side of the dog before moving to the other. Keep working down and around the neck and shoulder area, blending the shortest hair along the underside of the neck gradually into the longer hair on the sides and top of the neck.

Note that the hair growth around the neck tends to be rather heavy, no doubt to protect the jugular vein from attack. As a result, your work here will take some time, judiciously tipping and thinning this density, to avoid that heavily tipped or bunchy-coated look. Continue to work your shears along the sides, constantly looking back to what you have already trimmed, to check the smoothness from that angle.

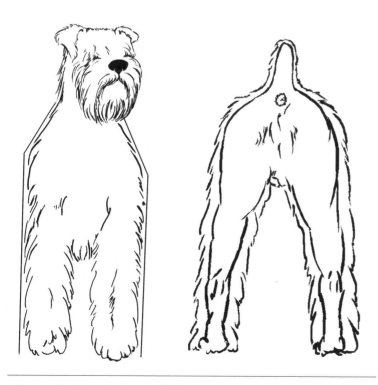

Correct trim from the front and the rear.

Check the topline by back combing. You will need to do somewhat more tipping around the withers, as the coat here tends to part and hang. You will need to do some thinning along the top of the loin areas, as the coat here tends to be thicker and bunchy. Remember, tipping the entire topline will make the coat stand up and you will be left with areas that look as though your dog has a crew-cut. This will not be compatible with the longer coat on the sides and will detract from the more natural look which is the desired effect.

Continue shortening and blending the coat along the croup and on the tail. Take care not to remove too much hair from the front of the base of the tail. Here again, you must blend the longer coat on the back to the base of the tail, and shorten the coat more toward its tip. Clean off the back of the tail, but keep in mind that you do not want the entire tail cleaned of coat, as it will resemble a pencil sticking out of a haystack.

DON'T OVERTRIM

Having done your work along the neck, shoulders, and the topline to croup and tail, check your work by grasping a small amount of hair between your thumb and forefinger on the other side of your dog. Pull the coat downward, then release the pressure (but not your grasp). Pull down and release again a few times, to create a rolling motion on the dog's side. This will "pop" the coat along the topline and side, allowing you to check your work. Beware of over trimming! The more you shorten the hair, the more it will pop, so use the thinning technique to minimize popping. Tidy any stray wisps, if necessary.

The sides of the dog down to the tuck-up should carry gradually longer coat. There will be less tipping and more thinning as you move downward. This will create a more natural look—the basic idea of blending.

Trim in the line of the brisket and tuck-up. A gentle curving line under the body is visually pleasing on a terrier. The coat should be the longest at the elbow, gradually sloping upward to the loin, creating the tuck-up and curving down again to blend with the hair on the stifle. Too little or too much tuck-up will destroy the proper balance of the dog.

Again we want this to look natural, so do not cut across and make a "skirt" of hair all of the same length. Point the shears down and at an angle toward the far side of the dog. Thin the coat when necessary, by using shears under the dog, pointing up toward the dog's underside.

LEGS AND FEET

Legs and feet are the next objective. The Soft Coated Wheaten Terrier's front legs should appear as columns and a continuation of a straight line from the jowl, down the neck and chest. The columnar effect is achieved by a slight flare of the coat below the knees and taper of coat back to the foot.

The coat needs a tight trim around the toes to give the "up on the toes" look desired in most terriers. To trim feet, start by placing scissors flat on the table, under excess hair with the inside blade laying close to the foot. Open the blade, then tilt slightly so the outside blade rises from the table, and the inside blade is still on the table next to the foot. Proceed to cut around the circumference of the foot, removing any "snow shoe" effect. Tidy stray hairs, and tighten the circumference of the foot by using the blades at a greater angle from the table. Switch to thinning shears and round out the toe area.

Fluff comb the leg and, with thinning shears pointing in the same direction that the coat would normally lay (either down or up), trim off excess in a columnar effect, retaining the slight flare around the base of the leg. Thinning may be required in the area of the elbow where hair can be more dense, and also on the inside of the leg from the knee down. Remember to work around the circumference of the leg for the columnar effect.

To check your work, pick up the leg by the toes, and shake it. This will "pop" the coat. Tip and thin areas that do not lay correctly. Thin out bunchy areas. Don't try to tip them shorter. Work in a constantly moving arc around each leg, to check all views of your column.

The rear legs are more complex in shape, due to the joints at the hock, stifle, and pelvis (pin-bones). Your object is to set in this angulation with trimming. The line indicating the stifle should be a gentle curve from the loin area to the front of the hock joint where it drops straight down to the toes. The hair covering the leg from the hock to the ground should form a cylinder when viewed from any angle. It should be perpendicular to the ground. Be careful not to trim more than a perpendicular angle from hock to ground as this creates the impression the dog has sickle-hocks.

On the rear, trim so that there is an indication of the pin bones. Be careful not to remove too much coat here, or to leave too much of an indication, thereby creating a "shelf," an exaggeration to be avoided. Trim straight down from the pin-bones to the second thigh (back of the stifle joint) and trim the second thigh, following the natural slope or angulation, to the point of the hock.

From the rear, create a straight line on the inside of the rear legs by cleaning out the hair between the legs. More hair can be removed where the legs join the body, as the hair forms a "skirt" here, but be careful not to remove so much coat as to expose the skin. The hair will be left longer along the inside of the second thigh to the hock, to create a straight line. Thin the coat from the hock down to the ground.

On the outside of the rear legs, the hair forms "bloomers" over the hip and down to the second thigh, as it grows more densely here. This area requires a bit more tipping than thinning. However, some thinning is needed to avoid the scissored or sculpted look on the hips. The fluff-combing technique is useful here, as it will simulate the pop of the coat when the dog moves. Make sure that you move around the dog's rear to the side occasionally to check what needs blending from the rear to the side coat. You want to "round off" the corners between these two angles. Pick up the rear leg by the toes and shake it to see what areas need further tidying.

GROOMING THE HEAD

The last area to tackle is the head. Start by cleaning excess hair off the ears. Holding the edge of the ear between your thumb and fingers; using your fingers as edge guides, trim the hair around the edge of the ear closely with straight blade scissors. Be sure to always point the scissors toward the tip of the ear, to minimize the possibility of cutting it. Clean off the hair on the inside of the flap with straight blade scissors or an electric clipper.

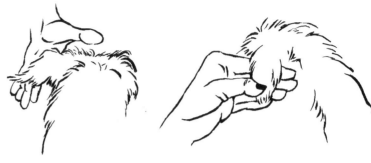

The correct way to hold the ear when trimming.

With thinning shears, trim the hair on the outside leather. Hold the shears to point up toward the fold. It is helpful to lay the ear on the flat of your hand for support. The hair should be trimmed closely on the lower third of the ear. As you trim higher along the leather, allow the shears to head up and away from the leather, to gradually lengthen the hair. The hair at the fold should be left at least one third of an inch long.

Stand at the side of the dog's head, fluff comb the coat on the skull from the occiput to the brow (approximately a half inch above the eye). Lay the shears PARALLEL to the plane of the dog's profile and trim in a straight line to coat on top of the skull. Now stand at the front of the dog and trim the top of the skull coat, blending it with the coat length on the fold of the ears. Carefully blend the coat at the occiput area in with the neck coat. Take care not to leave too much coat on the topknot, or not enough coat on the ears.

With thinning shears, thin out carefully down between the eyes in a V-shaped area, to remove the extra hair over and between the eyes that would obstruct the straight plane you wish to create from occiput to nose. The cheeks require thinning in a straight plane from the ears to the corner of the eyes. This area needs to be rather clean, but beware of over trimming or there will not be enough coat for blending.

To blend properly, allow the hair to get longer as you approach the corner of the eye. It may be necessary to thin or tip a bit down the lower side of the muzzle and into the beard in order to accomplish the desired flat plane along the cheek. The hair in the corner where the skull and cheek planes meet should be removed at a 45° angle. Tip this area from the ear down to the brow and CAREFULLY over the eye. The eye should be indicated only by judicious thinning of the forelock. The eye should never be completely exposed or have a visor of hair over it.

As a finishing touch, thin out under the jowl area and toward the beard, again creating a straight line from the jowl to the point of the beard. You may need to thin, shorten and/or shape the beard with the use of the thinning/tipping technique. Now, check the dog while he is standing on the ground. Have someone stack the dog in show stance. Then have your helper

Correct and incorrect head trims from the side and the top.

Incorrect—thinning not carried far enough down cheeks and skull.

Incorrect—eyebrows evident, beard too full.

Incorrect—thinning not carried far enough down cheeks and skull.

Areas for closer trimming on the neck.

Diagram of a properly trimmed Wheaten.

move the dog. Trim away any hair that obscures or distorts leg movement, topline or any part of the dog.

COAT LENGTH

It is not possible to give the actual length of coat that would be left on any given area of any dog. The individual dog's coat and structure will be the determining factors. For example, change in coat texture and quality as the dog matures will require

you to trim differently to achieve the desired results. A drop in the chest when the dog matures, will necessitate more coat being removed in this area. The objective of the trimming is to create a similar product from varied elements.

To reiterate, it is important that you have a mental image of what you wish to create. The goal in trimming a Wheaten properly is to NATU-RALIZE your trimming by the combined thinning/tipping process. Naturally stylish is the desired effect, not unnaturally stylized!

Ch. Hilltop's Ain't Misbehavin', owned, bred and handled by Beverly Streicher, is shown here winning an Award of Merit under breeder judge Gwynne McNamara at the 1995 National Specialty. This highly coveted win is the reward for the hard work and extra effort put into grooming and conditioning a Wheaten into winning form. (photo by John Ashbey)

Ch. Mellickway Crackerjack completing his championship under Dr. M. Josephine Deubler at Montgomery County 1974 at age six and a half months, a breed record. His owner Sherry Yanow handled him. "Rory" had a successful show career that included a Group placement at the International K.C. of Chicago in 1975. Note the amount of coat the dog carries compared to current styles. (photo by Evelyn Shafer)

CHAPTER 10

The Working Wheaten

Living with a well-behaved dog who is under his owner's control at all times is one of the most plea-surable sides of the human/canine connection. A dog who will sit, stay and come on command makes your life easier and his life as well. These commands and habits should be so ingrained that the dog responds to them instantly. A fast response to a command in an emergency can often save a dog's life.

As the first domesticated animals, dogs enjoy a special relationship with humankind. Basically, dogs want to do our bidding because they love to please their human masters. Unfortunately, most people do not realize that in order for the dog to please us, we have to let the dog know what we expect of him. Communication between dog and owner is not easy. We inadvertently train our dogs to behave both well and badly.

Some breeds are more trainable than others. Soft Coated Wheatens tend to be easier to train than many other terriers, but they are still not as tractable as a Golden Retriever or a German Shepherd Dog. To be successfully trained, they need a firm but gentle hand.

WHY TRAIN?

One advantage of obedience training the Wheaten is that the dog and his/her owner develop a rapport that greatly enhances the quality of the relationship. Nothing cements this unique partnership like learning together. Dogs operate by way of a pack mentality. When the owner takes the role of pack leader, the dog develops respect for him or her. When the dog is the pack leader, the owner lives in a

Betsy Geertson tracking with one of her Wheatens.

state of fear and uncertainty in the shadow of a canine dictator.

A well-behaved Wheaten is a good advertisement for the breed. A trained dog is a welcome neighbor. It is to the owner's benefit to take the time and make the effort required to teach his/her dog basic obedience.

Competition in performance events is an activity that the whole family can enjoy. Joining an Obedience club is a way to socialize with people and dogs. Getting "hooked" on training can lead to all kinds of rewards including titles, friendships and well-behaved, manageable dogs.

One of the major duties of the AKC approved Obedience clubs is to conduct training classes. The AKC can help you locate such clubs in your area. The classes given by these clubs are based on the AKC requirements for the various Obedience titles. The exercises gradually increase in difficulty and complexity as one advances from one title to the next.

AKC OBEDIENCE TITLES

In order to acquire an AKC Obedience title, a dog must earn three qualifying scores or "legs" under three different judges in AKC-sanctioned Obedience Trials. To get a qualifying score, a dog must earn more than half of the points in each exercise and get a final total of 170 points or better.

The titles a dog may earn are: Companion Dog (CD), Companion Dog Excellent (CDX), Utility Dog (UD), Utility Dog Excellent (UDX) and Obedience Trial Champion (OTCH). The two Tracking titles are Tracking Dog (TD) and Tracking Dog Excellent (TDX). Except for the

OTCH, the abbreviations for Obedience titles follow the dog's name. Only the highest title attained appears. Thus when a dog earns a CDX title, the CD is no longer used. The ultimate Obedience title is the achievement of an OTCH and a TDX. The dog's name would then show in Obedience Trial catalogs as OTCH (dog's name) TDX.

The first tier in Obedience Trials is the Novice level. Here dogs work for the CD degree. The exercises and scores in the Novice classes are:

1. Heel on leash and figure eight	40 points
2. Stand for examination	30 points
3. Heel free	40 points
4. Recall	30 points
5. Long sit	30 points
6. Long down	30 points
Total	200 points

The second tier in Obedience Trials is the Open level. Here dogs work for the CDX degree. The exercises and scores in the Open classes are:

1. Heel free and figure eight	40 points
2. Drop on recall	30 points
3. Retrieve on flat	20 points
4. Retrieve over high jump	30 points
5. Broad jump	20 points
6. Long sit	30 points
7. Long down	30 points
Total	200 points

In the Open classes the long sit and down are conducted with handlers out of sight.

The third tier in Obedience Trials is the Utility level. Here dogs work for the challenging UD degree. The exercises and scores in the Utility class are:

1. Signal exercise	40 points	
2. Scent discrimination article #1	30 points	
3. Scent discrimination article #2	30 points	
4. Directed retrieve	30 points	
5. Moving stand and examination	30 points	
6. Directed jumping	40 points	
Total	200 points	

The weave pole exercise is another part of Agility competition. (photo courtesy of Betsy Geertson)

A dog with a UD title may continue to compete. If he obtains qualifying scores in both Open and Utility classes at ten different AKC Obedience Trials, he can earn the UDX title.

The OTCH title can be obtained only after a dog has earned a UD title. The dog continues to participate in Open and/or Utility classes. The title requires the dog to earn 100 points and the point schedule is determined by the class, Open or Utility, and the number of dogs competing. Points are earned for first and second place wins. For example, if a dog takes first in a Utility class with ten to fourteen dogs competing, he gets six points. As you can see, it is not an easy task for a dog to become an OTCH.

Tracking Tests are held as separate events. A dog either passes or not. A track is laid and the dog is scored on how well he follows the trail and locates an article that was dropped by the track layer. The TDX track is longer and more difficult

The see-saw exercise is part of Agility Tests. (photo courtesy of Betsy Geertson)

Am., Can. Ch. Legenderry Spectator Sport, CGC, Am., Can. CD, was the earliest recorded Soft Coated Wheaten Terrier to become a Canine Good Citizen. (photo by Kathleen Moyer)

Gramachree's Minute Man, CDX, the first Soft Coated Wheaten Terrier to win an AKC Obedience title. (photo by Master Craft)

than the first level track. Many Wheatens have obtained tracking titles—a proud achievement for the breed.

Agility

Agility is a performance activity that AKC has recently approved as a competitive event at AKC shows and trials. In Agility Tests a dog must proceed through an obstacle course. Scoring is based on the time the dog takes to complete it. The classes are Novice Agility, Open Agility and Agility Excellent. The Novice class is divided into divisions A and B. The first is for persons and dogs who have never acquired an Agility title. The titles that can be won are Novice Agility (NA), Open

Calling upon long-dormant instincts, this Wheaton shows its style as a herding dog. (photo by Judy Price)

Agility (OA), Agility Excellent (AX) and Master Agility Excellent (MX). To acquire a title, a dog must have qualifying scores in three trials under at least two different judges. A qualifying score is eighty-five out of a possible one hundred points without a non-qualifying deduction. Times are counted in hundredths of a second. Courses become longer and more difficult as the dog progresses from Novice through the higher classes.

Agility Testing is a fast-moving and exciting activity. Dogs jump through rings, over bars, run through tunnels, climb ladders and negotiate a see-saw. Once a dog has his basic obedience training, Agility Tests can be fun for the whole family.

The American Kennel Club developed its Canine Good Citizen test in September, 1989. The purpose is to demonstrate that a dog can be trained to behave at home and in public. It is a non-competitive certification program in which the dog is evaluated on a pass/fail basis. There are ten tests, and the dog must pass them all. All tests are done on leash and involve everyday occurrences in a dog's life. Many Wheatens have been certified as CGCs.

Another certification program is run by an organization called Therapy Dogs International. As in the CGC certification, dogs are evaluated on their ability to react properly in various kinds of situations. Certified Therapy Dogs visit hospitals and nursing homes on a regular basis. It has been proven that petting a dog lowers a person's blood

Glimeren Glee Daisy CD, owned by John and Heather Giles, is a Certified Therapy dog as well as being Herding Instinct Certified. (photo by Heather Giles)

pressure. Visits from a well-behaved, well-groomed Wheaten can brighten the day for the sick and aged alike. It is an extremely useful and worthwhile thing to do with your dog and Wheatens have proven themselves more than equal to the demands of the work.

Wheatens are not eligible to participate in AKC approved herding events. Even so, a number of Wheatens have been recognized as having herding instincts at trials run by other organizations. If you live in an area where herding activities and tests are available, be brave and give it a try. Remember, Wheatens were originally bred as all-around farm dogs.

The more things you do with your dog, the closer your relationship will be. Make your dog part of your daily activities by taking him on errands, and even vacations if you go to a suitable place where a dog is an acceptable guest. Above all, enjoy your dog.

SOME SUCCESS STORIES

Wheatens have been acquiring Obedience titles since the 1960s, when the O'Connors became interested in obedience training. Margaret's sister, Eileen, trained Gramachree's Minute Man to his CD title in 1964. "Rory" was the first of the breed to gain an AKC Obedience title and got his CDX in 1966.

In 1965 at the age of eight and a half years, Holmenock's Gramachree became the first Wheaten bitch to get a CD. The O'Connors also put CD titles on Gramachree's Little Firecracker and Faraderry Fairy in 1966. Gramachree's Paisteen Fionn finished her CD in 1968 and Faraderry Fairy became a CDX in 1969.

Another Gramachree-bred dog, Gramachree's Roderick Dhu, CD (Gramachree's Minute Man, CDX ex Faraderry Fairy, CDX) was trained by owner Suzanne Bobley to his CD title in 1968. Max, as he was called, was the foundation of the Maxwell line. Max appeared with Mia Farrow and Dustin Hoffman in the 1969 film *John and Mary*.

Andover Dancing up a Storm was High in Trial at the first SCWTCA licensed Obedience Trial with a score of 171. Also pictured (left to right) Pam Donohue, President; Carol Carlson, Show Chairman; Sharla Walstrom, owner and judge Rev. Thomas O'Connor.

Max also appeared on the well-known children's television show, *Captain Kangaroo*.

The first Soft Coated Wheaten Terrier to become a UD was Rian's Captain Casey (Gramachree's Deoch an Dorais ex Holmenock's Hascara) in 1980. In 1982 Templemore Silk `N` Ribbons, UD (Ch.Erinmore's Gleanngay Charley ex Ch. Gleanngay's Gwyneth) became the second UD Wheaten.

In 1984, Moonstar Tory, UD finished her Utility and TDX titles. She is the first Wheaten in the United States with both titles and has Canadian Obedience titles as well.

Winterberry's Graceful Tracy, UDX, the first Soft Coated Wheaten Terrier to win this advanced title. (photo by Glenda Krueger)

Ch. Legenderry Baby Snooks (Can., Am. Ch. Jamboree Gleanngay Gaucho ex Ch. Legenderry Babe In the Woods, ROM) has her CDX and TDX titles, as well as championships in both Canada and the United States. She also has six champion get. Ch. Hollywood's Happy Jack, UDX (Riverrun Peregrin Took ex Riverrun's Hollywood Debut, CD) also has Canine Good Citizen, Therapy Dog and Herding Instinct certification. This dog has been placed High in Trial on many occasions.

The above Wheatens are mentioned as examples of great Obedience Trial successes. The breed has yet to record the first Wheaten OTCH, but that too will come about in due course. There are many Wheaten Therapy Dogs and Canine Good Citizens. A Wheaten once played the role of Sandy in a production of the musical comedy, *Annie*. We should all greatly admire those Wheaten owners who have achieved so much working with and training their dogs.

Obedience training is beneficial for all dogs, large or small. All the dogs used in advertising and movies started with basic obedience training. There is no excuse for not teaching your dog to behave well. Earning a title is the icing on the cake.

Headliners

The dedicated hobby breeder's goal is to produce animals who come as close as possible to the blueprint of the ideal Soft Coated Wheaten Terrier as set forth in the breed Standard. Part and parcel of achieving that goal involves exhibiting the dogs he or she has bred. A great deal of thought and knowledge goes into each breeding. One of a breeder's fondest dreams is to breed that elusive Best in Show dog. Another is to have one's breeding stock included on the SCWTCA's Register of Merit—a most coveted award given to dogs who produce a minimum of fifteen champions and bitches who produce a minimum of eight champions.

In this chapter we will look at Wheatens who were successful in the conformation ring and as top producers in the years since 1973 when the Wheaten was first recognized, with the emphasis on the last ten to fifteen years. As history is a continuum, it is difficult to decide upon clear demarcations, especially since some of the early breeders still exert a significant influence on the Wheaten.

FOUR MAJOR WHEATEN LINES

It is important to remember that American Wheaten pedigrees all trace back to a small number of dogs imported from Ireland and England in the 1960s. In turn, most of the dogs in the ring today trace back to four major lines that were established in that period. They are: Amaden (Emily Holden and Carol Carlson), Andover (Jackie Gottlieb and Cindy Vogels), Gleanngay (Gay Dunlap) and Waterford (Marjorie Shoemaker). These prefixes continue to acquire glory in today's show ring. It is interesting to note that all the aforementioned ladies were introduced to Wheatens by Anne Elwell, an early fancier who used Slievehoven as her prefix. It is readily apparent that a relatively small number of dogs and breeders have set the mold for the Wheaten in the United States. This influence continues as the descendants of these important dogs make their own mark in Wheaten history.

Amaden

The Amaden prefix, owned by Emily Holden and Carol Carlson, is one of the oldest still active Wheaten lines. Emily and Carol started their breeding program with dogs from several different families at a time when there was not a great deal of choice in viable breeding stock.

Carol owned Ballymoor Heather (Cobalt Bourcro Ballybay ex Cornbin Tanjareen) and Roscommon's Uncommon (Gallagher of Sunset Hill ex Mocara of Sunset Hill). She was bred to Brenock's Kelly's Lucky Charm (Binheath Perro Benito ex Little Mermaid of the Egerluk) and produced Emily's foundation bitch, Jenny Love of Addison Mews. Emily also acquired Amaden's Katie Love (Dungarvin of Sunset Hill ex Brydie of Balitara) from Anne Elwell and later owned Brydie, who was by Benker Belton out of Gramachree's Eivlin Aruin.

This was the beginning of an enduring partnership. In 1971 Carol and Emily imported Irish Ch. Benmul Belma (Holmenock's Hancock ex Hurley's Lass), who became the second Wheaten champion. They then embarked on a breeding program that began with a mating between Jenny

Ch. Amaden's Leading Man, ROM, bred and owned by Emily Holden. (photo by Chuck Tatham)

Love and Ch. Koop's Kilkenny of Woodridge, ROM (Ch. Abby's Postage Dhu o'Waterford, ROM ex O'Hagan's Cindy of Ashworth). A bitch from that mating, Ch. Amaden's Rainbow's End, was bred to Ch. Templemore Marathon Man (Ch. Gleanngay Holliday, ROM ex Ch. Gleanngay's Gwyneth) and produced Ch. Amaden's Tess of Marabow, who was then bred back to Holliday. One of the resulting bitches, Ch. Amaden's Kate of Marabow, was a Terrier Group winner as well as a top producer.

Rainbow's End, bred to Holliday, produced five champions, one of whom, Ch. Amaden's Abby Holliday, was bred back to her sire. This mating produced Ch. Amaden's Leading Man, one of Amaden's most successful show dogs as well as a top producer.

Ch. Koop's Kilkenny of Woodridge winning Best of Opposite Sex at the 1976 National Specialty under judge Mrs. James E. Clark, Penny Belviso, handler. (photo by William Gilbert)

In more recent years, Emily has imported some dogs from Ireland in an effort to enlarge the gene pool in the United States. Other breeders are also importing dogs from Great Britain and the continent. Their influence on American Wheatens has yet to be determined.

Andover

Andover Wheatens is the kennel prefix used by Jackie Gottlieb and her daughter, Cindy Vogels.

Ch. Andover Song and Dance Man, ROM (Ch. Gleanngay Holliday, ROM ex Ch. Andover Hootenanny, ROM) compiled an enviable show record. He won the national Specialty show at Montgomery County four times (once from the Veterans Class), two SCWTCA roving Specialties and eleven local Specialty events. In addition to these awards, he won five all-breed Bests in Show and the Terrier Group at Westminster in 1989,

Ch Andover Song 'n' Dance Man, ROM, owned by Cindy Vogels winning the Terrier Group at the 1989 Westminster Kennel Club show under judge William Bergum. "Harry" won five all-breed Bests in Show and a host of Specialty Bests. (photo by John Ashbey)

Ch. Stephen Dedalus of Andover, CD, ROM, bred and owned by Jackie Gottlieb, was one of the breed's most influential sires following AKC recognition. Many American pedigrees trace back to him.

making him the first and thus far the only Wheaten to have become a Westminster Group winner. He is the top winning Wheaten in history as of this writing.

Jackie and Cindy also bred Ch. Stephen Dedalus of Andover CD, ROM (Leprecaun's Jackeen Arrah ex Andover Antic of Sunset Hill, CD), one of the watershed dogs in Wheaten history. Many top kennels began with "Sweeney's" offspring. His littermate, Cissy Caffrey of Andover, produced Ch. Glenworth Andover Answer, ROM, the Gottliebs' top producing bitch. Cindy Vogels

owned Ch. Raclee Express West O'Andover CD, ROM (Ch. Glenworth's Country Squire, ROM ex Ber., Am. Ch. Racleee's Serendipity), who was otherwise known as Ryan. Ryan is the grandsire of the Westminster Group winner, Ch. Andover Song'n'Dance Man, ROM (Harry).

Ryan, whose photo appears at the beginning of this chapter, was also the sire of Ch. Briarlyn Dandelion, ROM out of Ch. Kenwoods Abby O'Briarlynn and traces back to Sweeney through both his sire and dam. Dandelion won four consecutive SCWTCA Specialty shows in 1977 and 1978—two rovings and two nationals. He was used extensively at stud and produced fifty-five champions before his accidental death in 1981. Nearly half of his offspring were top producers. One can only wonder at what his impact would have been had he achieved a normal life span.

Harry, when bred to Ch. Doubloon's Illusion in 1989, produced Ch. Doubloon's Master of Illusion, who was also a multiple Group and Specialty winner. A repeat of the breeding produced another notable winner, Ch. Andover All Done With Mirrors.

A dog like Harry may come along only once in a lifetime, but his appearance was not a fluke. It was the result of twenty years of careful, planned breeding. His influence will continue to be felt as time goes on.

Gleanngay

The Gleanngay line belongs to Gay S. Dunlap. It began with the purchase of Ch. Innisfree's Annie Sullivan, ROM (O'Callahan of Sunset Hill ex

Ch. Briarlyn Dandelion, ROM, won the Roving and National Specialties in 1977 and 1978. He was owned and shown by Lynne Penniman and is pictured in 1978 at his fourth Specialty Best under judge Anne Marie Moore. (photo by John Ashbey)

Croomboor Crackerjill) in 1970. Annie became the third Wheaten champion in 1973. She produced twenty champions, five of whom became top producers. She earned a permanent place in breed history when she became the first Wheaten to win an all-breed Best in Show on St. Patrick's Day in 1974 at the Tidewater KC.

From a breeding point of view Gay's most important dog was Ch. Gleanngay Holliday, ROM

(Ch. Koop's Kilkenny of Woodridge, ROM ex Ch. Gleanngay Goldilach, ROM). Here was another watershed dog ready to join the ranks of other significant sires including Ch. Stephen Dedalus of Andover CD, ROM, Ch. Abby's Postage Dhu O'Waterford, ROM (the first Wheaten champion)

Ch Gleanngay Holliday, ROM, bred and owned by Gay Dunlap, was a significant stud force in the Wheaten. His name appears in the pedigrees of many of the breed's top winners in the ring today. (photo by John Ashbey)

and his own sire. Gay called him "Doc." Marjorie Shoemaker called him the "cure for the common Wheaten."

Gay has always considered herself a breeder first and an exhibitor second. She certainly recognized the need for her dogs to compete in the breed ring, but she also realized that she could not do it all. Thus, she has selectively sold dogs to people who have subsequently become successful breeders and exhibitors themselves.

Janet Turner Dalton began with Ch. Gleanngay Gotta Be Me (Ch. Abby's Postage Dhu, ROM ex Ch. Innisfree's Annie Sullivan, ROM). Since she started her Wildflower line, she has had immense success. Ch. Wildflower Woodbalm (Ch. Briarlyn Dandelion, ROM ex Ch. Gleanngay Gotta be Me) won the national Specialty in 1980. Ch. Wildflower Star Dust, ROM (Ch. Gleanngay Gather Moondust ex Ch. Gleanngay Gotta Be Me) was a multiple Specialty winner. Wildflower dogs are consistently well represented in SCWTCA's list of Top Producers.

Candy Way started her Bantry Bay line with Ch. Gleanngay Holly Berry (Ch. Gleanngay Holliday, ROM ex Gleanngay She's the Berries). Her son, Ch. Bantry Bay Gleanngay Kashmir, ROM out of Ch. Gleanngay Gather Moondust, ROM was a Best in Show and multiple Specialty winner. A repeat of the breeding produced Ch. Bantry Bay Kairo, ROM, who won the national Specialty in 1990 and had many Group placements. Kashmir bred to Ch. Amaden's Whistling Dixie (Ch. Gleanngay Holliday ROM ex Amaden's Tess of Marabow) produced Am., Can. Ch.

Ch. Bantry Bay Gleanngay Kashmir, ROM, bred and owned by Candy Way, was a Best in Show and multiple Specialty winner. (photo by Alverson Photographers)

Amaden's Kash Sterling, who also had a successful show career.

Ch. Bantry Bay Tov Natan (Ch. Kairi's Kaluha ex Ch. Bantry Bay Ronnie Mcdonnie) is the latest in a long line of Group placing dogs bred by Candy Way.

Ch. Bantry Bay Kairo, ROM, was Best of Breed at the 1990 National Specialty. (photo by John Ashbey)

"Casey" became the first Wheaten champion and proved truly important to the subsequent development of the breed. Major Waterford influence comes through Casey and he appears in the pedigrees of a majority of the champions finished during the mid-1970s. Marjorie showed his son, Ch. Koop's Kilkenny of Woodridge out of O'Hagan's Cindy of Ashworth to his championship. "Koop" was widely used at stud, and as noted earlier in this chapter, produced Ch. Gleanngay Holliday, ROM. Casey became the number one Terrier sire in 1975 and 1976 based on the number of his champion sons and daughters. He truly left his mark on the breed.

Waterford

The last, but not least, of the four major lines that began in the 1970s is Waterford. Dan and Marjorie Shoemaker selected that name as their kennel prefix. Their first Wheaten was a male, Glocca Morra's Ian Harrigan, CDX (Callahan of Sunset Hill ex Longridge Eileen Aroon). Two bitches, Ch. Cloverlanes Connaught, CD (Gramachree's Dermod O'Derry ex Thistledown of the Egerluk) and Dena of Waterford (Dungarvin of Sunset Hill ex Gilchrist Gal O'Slievehoven) were added to the Waterford household. In 1972 Marjorie purchased Ch. Abby's Postage Dhu O'Waterford, ROM (Ch. Stephen Dedalus of Andover, CD, ROM ex Berdot's Brigette).

Ch. Abby's Postage Dhu O'Waterford, ROM, the breed's first champion, owned by Marjorie Shoemaker. (photo by William Gilbert)

In 1980 Ch. Lontree's Borstal Boy, ROM (Ch. Raclee Express West O'Andover, ROM ex Ch. Waterford Lontree Lace, ROM) won an all-breed Best in Show, the first of two, making him the first Wheaten to do so since 1974. He was owner-handled by Gary Vlachos and bred by Joy Laylon. As did Marjorie Shoemaker, Joy began her Lontree line with a Cloverlane dog. In addition to Borstal Boy, Joy bred Ch. Lontree's Star Waggin, ROM, who won the national Specialty in 1984.

He placed in numerous Groups and won other Specialty shows.

Lontree dogs were used by Gary Vlachos and Bill Behan when they began their Brenmoor line. A grandson of Borstal Boy, Ch Brenmoor's Spark Plug was also a multiple Best in Show and Specialty winner and placed in the top ten Wheaten list in 1988, 1989 and 1990. Gary is licensed to judge Wheatens at AKC shows. Other Wheaten breeders who have become eligible to

Ch. Lontree's Borstal Boy winning Best in Show under judge H. Lee Huggins at the Alamance (NC) KC in 1980. This was the first Best in Show for a Wheaten since Ch. Innisfree's Annie Sullivan "broke the ice" at the Tidewater KC on Saint Patrick's Day 1974. (photo by Graham/Bonnie)

Ch. Brenmoor's Spark Plug went Best in Show at the Butler County (PA) show in 1988 under judge Eleanor Evers, handled by Allison Corn. This was his second top award.

judge are Gay Dunlap, Sue Goldberg, Gwynne McNamara, Dan Shoemaker, Cindy Vogels and Candy Way.

THE NEW STARS

Every exhibitor's dream is to win an all-breed Best in Show award. Wheatens don't achieve this goal as often as other terriers, but the breed is beginning to acquire moderate success at winning the top award. In addition to the others already mentioned, Am., Can. Ch. Marima's Classical Jazz, ROM (Ch. Briarlyn Kris Kringle ex Marima's Apple Brandee) won two Bests in Show in 1984. He was owned by Mary Lou Lafler, and his lineage goes back to Sweeney through his sire and through his great-great grandsire on his dam's side, Ch. Mellickway Crackerjack, ROM (Ch. Stephen Dedalus of Andover CD, ROM ex Lady Patricia of Windmill), bred by the author.

Another of Mary Lou Lafler's dogs, Ch. Marima's Easy Money (Ch. Wildflower Snapdragon, ROM ex Ch Marima's Keepsake) won two Bests in Show in 1988 and in 1989.

In the 1980s and 1990s new kennel names filled the ranks of top winners and top producers. Beverly Mac Donald started her Greentree line with a bitch from Marjorie Shoemaker, Ch. Waterford Red Rose, ROM (Ch. Briarlyn Dandelion ROM ex Ch. Cloverlanes's Connaught, CD). "Rose" was bred to Ch. Gleanngay Holliday, ROM and produced Ch. Greentree Man O'Waterford, ROM. Ch. Greentree Alysheba (Ch. Webspinner Tour de Force ex Ch. Greentree Shibui Santa Anita) is a recent star from the

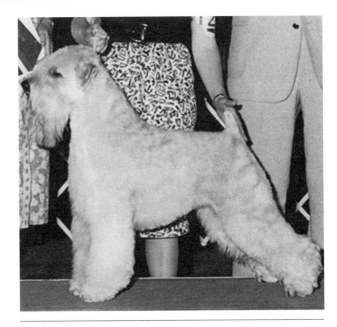

Ch. Marima's Easy Money won a Best in show in 1988. He was the second Best in Show winner bred by Mary Lou Lafler. The first was Am., Can. Ch. Marima's Classical Jazz, ROM. (photo by K. Kidd)

Greentree "stable." (Beverly often uses the names of race horses for her dogs.)

Susan Strange's Carlinayer line was based on Gleanngay stock. She started with three Gleanngay bitches. Her most successful dogs of this period were Ch. Carlinayer's Brendan Murdock (Ch. Carlinayer Man O'Gaeshill ex Ch. Carlinayer's Image O'Loveliness) and Ch. Carlinayer's Thru the Lookinglass (Ch. Wildflower Stardust ex Ch. Gleanngay Mirror Mirror, ROM). He was sent to Sweden, where he had a very creditable show career before returning to the United States.

Ch. Paisley After Midnight, owned by Kathleen and Evelyn McIndoe, winning the Terrier Group at the Durham KC under Mrs. Phyllis Haage, handled by Maripi Woolridge. (photo by John Ashbey)

Ch. Wildflower Stardust bred and owned by Janet Turner Dalton was a multiple Specialty winner at both the national and local levels. He is pictured winning the 1985 National under judge Barbara Keenan being handled by Maripi Woolridge. (photo by John Ashbey)

Shari Boyd Carusi started her career in junior showmanship, winning the SCWTCA's annual Junior Showmanship award for five consecutive years. She and her mother, Dee, started in Wheatens in 1985 with a bitch, Ch. Harvest's Double Holiday (Ch. Lontree Lasting Image O'Cully ex Harvest's Gold O'Crackerjack). In 1991, they bred a dog they named Ch. Shar-D's Let the Games Begin (Ch. Carlinayer's Stardust Image ex Ch Shar D's Winnin is Everything). He traces back to

Gleanngay through his sire and Andover through his dam. His successful show career included multiple Terrier Group and Best in Show wins and two national Specialties. He was the first Wheaten to place in the Terrier Group at the Montgomery County KC. This historic achievement came at the 1993 national Specialty with a second place. He went Best in Show at the 1993 Louisville KC, one of the largest all-breed shows in the United States.

The Legacy kennel prefix made its first appearance in 1990. Jon Caliri, Robert Hale and Janet Dalton co-owned Ch. Wildflower Peach Blossom (Ch. Windsong Rainbow's End, ROM ex Ch. Wildflower Dusty Rose). Ch. Legacy Moonlit

Knight, ROM (Ch. Wildflower Gold Dust, ROM ex Waterford Georgia Brown) was a top producer in 1992, 1993 and 1994. Ch. Legacy Wildwest Wildflower (Ch. Gleanngay Waggin Wheel ex Ch. Wildflower Peach Blossom) won the 1995 national Specialty.

Doubloon is one of the newer kennel names that became dominant in the mid–1980s. In 1983, Elena Landa obtained Am., Can. Ch. Legenderry Baby Snooks, Am., Can. CDX, TDX (Ch. Jamboree's Gleanngay Gaucho ex Ch. Legenderry's Babe in the Woods ROM) from Audrey Weintraub, one of the breed pioneers. Her great-grandson was Ch. Doubloon's Master of Illusion owned by Jackie

Gottlieb and Cindy Vogels who followed in his father's footsteps by winning an all-breed Best in Show and multiple Specialty shows. Ch. Doubloon's Expresso (Ch. Carlinayer's a Little Wiser ex Ch. Doubloon's Lasting Imprint) and his littermate, Ch. Doubloon's Happy Go Latte, both had outstanding show careers.

Ch. Shar-D's Let the Games Begin, bred and owned by Shari Boyd Carusi (handling) and Dee Boyd, was a multiple Best in Show and national Specialty winner and the first Wheaten to place in the Group at Montgomery County. He is shown here winning the Terrier Group at the Back Mountain KC under judge Seymour Weiss. (photo by Joe C)

Am., Can. Ch Wildflower Gold Dust, ROM, winning Best of Breed under Dr. Josephine Deubler at the Westminster KC show in 1988 for owner Kathy McIndoe, handled by Bill McFadden. (photo by John Ashbey)

Ch. Kaylinn's August Moon, owned and bred by Kay Baird-Zwier, was a 1997 Best in Show Winner. He was also Best of Breed at both the 1998 SCWTCA Roving Specialty and the Annual Specialty at Montgomery County where he went on to a Group third. (photo © Booth Photography)

Ch. Paisley Midnight Sun, owned by Kathleen, Margaret and Mary Evelyn McIndoe, taking Best in Show at the Mississippi Valley KC in 1996 under judge Kent Delaney, handled by Maripi Woolridge. (photo by Downey)

Ch. Doubloon's Happy Go Latte shown winning the Terrier Group at Whidbey Island in May 1994 under judge Robert Shreve. His breeder, Elena Landa, will most likely continue to build on the early success of her Doubloon line. (photo by Animal World Studio)

Ch. Kaylinn's August Moon (Ch. Carlinayer's Brendon Murdock ex Ch. Kaylinn's Sweet Clementine) won a Best in Show in 1998. His breeder-owner is Kay Baird-Zwier, who has been breeding Wheatens since the late 1980s.

The headliners discussed here illustrate how the four lines that dominated the 1970s continue to influence the breed today. As has already been noted, nearly all these recent winners trace their roots back to one or more of the following four lines: Amaden, Andover, Gleanngay and Waterford. Wheatens will likely change and hopefully continue to improve in the next decades, but surely the mold set in the 1970s will continue to be evident.

(photo © Dana Frady)

CHAPTER 12

What You Should Know About Breeding Dogs

Dog breeding is not a project to ever be undertaken lightly. The problem of unwanted pets in the United States today is overwhelming. Therefore, unless you feel you have a significant contribution to make to the betterment of the Soft Coated Wheaten Terrier, don't breed your dog!

At the present time about 2,000 Soft Coated Wheaten Terriers are registered with AKC each year. Magazines and newspapers often publish feature articles about the "best" dog or the "in" breed of the year. Wheatens appear in these articles more often than serious breeders would like. Currently, there is a great demand for Wheatens. However, the number of dedicated, conscientious breeders is not sufficient to produce enough Wheatens for everyone who wants one. It is, therefore, of the greatest importance that all responsible breeders inform the public about the disadvantages of the breed along with all the plus factors.

These same responsible breeders recognize that the breed's future depends on the decisions breeders make regarding which dogs to breed. They study pedigrees. They make an effort to see the ancestors of any dog to whom they are considering breeding or at least to locate pictures of those dogs. They know that they need ample time and sufficient, suitable space to raise a litter. They have the patience and the stamina to last through long hours of whelping and neonatal crises that often occur. They are members of SCWTCA and possibly a local Specialty club. Most of all, they are fully aware that only healthy Wheatens of superior conformation, and sound, stable temperament should be bred.

THE BREEDING PROCESS

Wheatens are generally easy to breed. Bitches tend to whelp freely and puppies have sufficient weight and substance to survive without heroic efforts. Only rarely are bitches reluctant mothers. Caesarean section is uncommon.

This chapter is not meant to give detailed instructions on breeding and whelping. Other sources provide excellent information on this subject. It is intended to give enough information to enable a new Wheaten owner to decide if breeding and the attendant work is worth it. It might also remind experienced breeders about their obligations to the breed.

When a person is deeply involved in a breed, it is only natural to proselytize about the breed's wonderful attributes to anyone who will listen, sometimes to great disadvantage. In the early days before recognition, owners were encouraged to breed their dogs just because they were Wheatens. AKC required sufficient numbers of dogs before it would consider a breed's acceptance, so those pioneers needed to work toward this.

In the late 1950s and 1960s dogs were bred who perhaps should not have been. At that time, the breed had not attracted what is known as the seasoned dog fraternity. Most true fanciers of the established terrier breeds tended to look down on this shaggy upstart; some still do. Few Wheaten owners had experience showing or breeding. Knowledgeable mentors were few and far between. By the 1970s, all of that had changed dramatically.

Today's Wheaten fancy is fortunate to have a core of dedicated, reputable breeders. Many have been active since the early days when everyone was still learning to play the dog game.

In a sense, the veterans within the breed have grown up, becoming wiser and more sophisticated. They now use contracts when selling puppies and require spay/neuter agreements. They are much more careful about which dogs are bred. Their breeding programs are well planned. It is this small but tenacious group that will assure the future success and progress in the breed by passing the essential knowledge to newcomers and continuing to follow these self-imposed high standards.

THE ECONOMICS OF BREEDING

Some people feel that they want to breed to recoup the purchase price of their dog. While Wheatens can be relatively expensive, if a buyer feels that she must get a payback by breeding, it might be better if she doesn't buy a Wheaten at all.

The expenses of raising a litter, as with everything else in our modern lives, are increasing. If your bitch is to be shipped to the stud dog of your choice, be aware that airline shipping has also become more costly in recent years. If you want to use your dog at stud, be prepared to spend the money needed to show him to his championship at the very least. Owners of bitches will not be lining up to use your dog unless he is a champion. They have plenty of champion stud dogs to choose from.

Veterinary costs have soared. Both stud dog and brood bitch must be checked for congenital eye defects, x-rayed for hip dysplasia and tested for brucellosis. Tail-docking, removal of dewclaws and inoculations add to the cost of raising a litter. If your litter should contract some kind of virus, in spite of expert medical care, the puppies may all die. Can you and your family deal with that kind of loss? You will still have to pay the stud fee and veterinary bills even if there are no puppies to sell.

Most hobby breeders do not advertise because the demand for Wheatens is so great and they often have a waiting list. Some do use specialized dog magazines in order to reach the audience for show dogs, but by and large, being a member of the national or local club gives a breeder sufficient exposure to prospective buyers. When you do find an advertisement in a newspaper, it is possible that the seller is a "backyard breeder" or a "front" for a commercial outlet.

WHY BREED?

Many people have the idea that it is necessary for a dog or bitch to be bred in order to be fulfilled. This is just not so. A male, once used for breeding, may begin to lift his leg to mark his "territory," which may possibly include your best furniture. He may wander and often becomes more aggressive with other males. Breeding a bitch just so she knows what motherhood is like makes no sense at all. In the wild, animals breed for survival of the species. In domesticated pets, this need is no longer critical.

Breeding so that your children can witness the miracle of birth is perhaps the worst reason to breed of all. Books with graphic illustrations of whelping are easy to find. Video cassettes are now available that show the birth of all types of animals. Whelping can be a long process and can entail episodes a child can find traumatic and disturbing. Few children can sit still for the extended periods of time between births and your bitch does not need an audience. Besides, most children are just not as interested as their parents might suppose.

THE WORK INVOLVED

There is no end of work to be done when you are raising a litter. Be prepared to sleep in the whelping room for a few nights. The first seven to ten days in a puppy's life are critical. A newborn puppy has no way of regulating his body temperature and must be kept in a room with an ambient temperature of at least 85° Fahrenheit.

Puppies need to be weighed every day for the first ten days. Nails have to be trimmed weekly. Nine puppies equal 36 wiggly little feet with 144 toes attached, a nail on each! If mama does not or cannot fulfill her duties, you will have to take over and tube or bottle feed the litter and stimulate each one to make sure they are eliminating.

If your bitch does her job well, you are home free until the puppies are weaned at about four weeks. At that point, mother no longer cleans up after her brood. You are then in charge, and it is a constant job to keep the puppy pen clean.

This is a time when members of your family may begin to resent this interruption in their routine. Spouses and children will demand that the puppy area be sanitized before they will venture anywhere near it. Puppies wake up with the birds, so reconcile yourself to early mornings.

When prospective buyers visit, you have to be there. Sometimes they will not show up at all. Again, your family will not be happy to give up their activities because you have to stay home with puppies.

When you are not caring for and cleaning up after the puppies, you have paperwork to complete—register the litter with AKC, prepare pedigrees, write up a complete set of detailed instructions, and prepare sales contracts. (Sample sales contracts are available from SCWTCA.) This, too, is a time-consuming job.

Breeders ordinarily spend an enormous amount of time on the telephone talking to people interested in Wheatens. It is incumbent on every breeder to be honest, polite and up-front about any dogs available for sale. Chances are that there will be more buyers than puppies. Eager buyers find it hard to understand why breeders don't have puppies when they call. This is when impatient potential Wheaten owners turn to other, less desirable sources of supply which, in turn, opens the door to commercial breeders.

If you are not discouraged by the awesome prospect of becoming a responsible breeder, this next section covers some of the things that you will actually have to do. It will briefly discuss the care of the bitch and stud before and after mating, the mating, whelping, and puppy care.

Theoretically, a puppy gets half of his genetic makeup from each parent. In reality, the bitch has more influence since fetal nourishment comes from her body and her maternal attitude affects that of the puppies. Ideally, the bitch will be healthy and mature, sound in mind and body, and free of major conformation faults.

INITIAL PREPARATION

Wheatens normally come into season about twice a year. A bitch should not be bred until her second season, and it is even better to wait until the third. If you have kept records of previous heats, you should know when to expect the next one. Bring your bitch's shots up to date and have your veterinarian perform a fecal analysis.

As close as possible to your bitch's season, have a brucellosis test performed. Brucellosis is a highly infectious, sterility-causing disease transmitted during breeding.

While hip dysplasia is not a major problem in the breed, your dog should be x-rayed to rule it out definitely. Your vet is most likely familiar with the procedure for submitting the x-rays to the Orthopedic Foundation for Animals for evaluation. The OFA ratings are as follows: 1–Excellent, 2–Good, 3–Fair, 4–Mild dysplasia, 5–Medium dysplasia, 6–Severe dysplasia. Only dogs with a rating of 3 or higher should be bred. Dogs with 4, 5 or 6 grades should be neutered or spayed. Permanent OFA numbers are only granted to dogs over the age of two years.

SCWTCA also accepts PennHip evaluations. This is the program under the auspices of the

University of Pennsylvania College of Veterinary Medicine in which dogs are evaluated at a much earlier age, which is an advantage for breeders.

Another necessary health check is an eye examination to determine whether progressive retinal atrophy (PRA) is present. This test must be performed by a canine ophthalmologist. The results are submitted to the Canine Eye Registry Foundation (CERF). If the eyes are clear of the disease, a number is granted. This test must be repeated annually.

It is vital that Wheaten breeders check their stock for these inherited disorders. By weeding out affected dogs before they are bred, conscientious breeders can help prevent the spread of these insidious conditions that have so seriously affected many other breeds.

The first signs of estrus, or heat as it is commonly known, is a swelling of the vulva that can be observed during routine grooming. Check the bitch daily for the first signs of a bloody discharge. Count the days of her season from that first flow. Some bitches keep themselves so clean that you may have to wipe the vulva with a cotton ball each day to be sure they are actually in season. Some breeders test with diabetes paper to determine when a bitch is ovulating. The size and softness of the vulva are indications of the progress of a bitch's season.

A season normally lasts about twenty-one days. This is often expressed as seven days coming, seven days in, and seven days going. Confine the bitch for the entire time she is in season, even after she has been bred. Leaving a bitch in season unsupervised in an outdoor run is not safe. Males have

been known to jump high fences to reach a female. I have even heard stories of dogs breeding through an opening in a crate. While your bitch is in heat, walk her on a leash and keep her confined at other times, preferably in her crate. It could be a tragedy if your bitch escaped through a door that was accidentally left open.

As soon as the bitch comes into season, have the vet test for vaginal infection. If one is present, there is still time to treat it before mating. All arrangements with the stud dog should have been made well in advance of the bitch's season. It is a good idea to have a back-up stud dog if for any reason your first choice is unavailable.

If you are shipping your bitch to the stud dog, time it so that she arrives at the rendezvous at the right time. Make the actual shipping arrangements at least forty-eight hours in advance, but consult the airline about its procedures long before your bitch comes into heat. Obtain an airline-approved crate and accustom your bitch to it well before the shipping date. Attach an envelope to the crate that contains a copy of the brucellosis test results, feeding instructions and whatever else the airline requires.

If you breed at the height of summer or in the depths of winter, you may have problems shipping. I am convinced that the airlines do not want to ship animals because they set up so many obstacles to such commerce. If you can find a suitable stud dog near enough for you to drive, you can save time and money while protecting your bitch from additional stress. (Using fresh chilled semen is an alternative that is discussed later.)

The owner of the stud dog also bears a responsibility to the breed. One of the most critical decisions a stud dog owner has to make is whether to breed to a particular bitch or not. It is not easy to turn down a stud fee. Breeding to a mediocre bitch doesn't enhance a dog's reputation. We are long past the time that every Wheaten who could be bred was, in fact, bred. Only those animals who are of outstanding quality with something to give to the breed ought to reproduce.

The stud dog also needs proper nutrition and veterinary care as discussed in regard to the brood bitch. The stud should be mature and healthy with no serious faults. The same health checks that apply to the bitch apply equally to the dog.

It is slightly more important for a stud to be a champion than for a bitch. All other things being equal, owners of bitches will prefer to use a dog who has been evaluated by at least three judges and has been found to be worthy of a championship title.

In a natural mating, the usual practice is to bring the bitch to the stud dog. This means that the owner of a stud dog has to have facilities to keep a bitch confined for as long as it takes to achieve the desired number of successful matings. Typically, as soon as the bitch is receptive, mating is done every other day until at least two successful breedings occur. If the bitch is being flown in from some distant point of origin, it is the stud dog owner's responsibility to pick her up at the airport and make arrangements for her to be shipped home.

The optimum time for mating is between the tenth and sixteenth days, but individual variation is quite routine. Most bitches will readily accept a male during that time. Of course, there will always be an occasional bitch who will resist all advances by the male even on optimum breeding days. Breeding my first bitch, Lady Patricia of Windmill, was always a struggle, but she conceived every time and was always an excellent mother.

The first time a dog is used at stud, it is better to match him to a bitch who has been bred before. This is no time to use a recalcitrant maiden who may injure a virgin male. Never simply close two dogs in a room by themselves and hope for the best. Have a helper and put both animals on leads. If the bitch seems snappish, muzzle her. Hold her firmly to allow the dog to mount her and begin thrusting. When the stud has achieved penetration and the penis enters the vagina, the bulb at its base becomes greatly enlarged and becomes locked in place by the action of the vaginal muscles. This is called the tie.

At this point the stud will normally dismount and turn so that he and bitch are eventually standing tail to tail. He may need assistance to turn safely. Do not let the bitch move or the male could be injured. After ejaculation the stud's erection will subside and he will withdraw from the bitch. Allow him to rest and, if necessary, gently help replace the sheath over his penis. Finally, crate the bitch and do not allow her to urinate for several hours.

ALTERNATIVE MATING METHODS

Artificial insemination is a procedure whereby semen is manually removed from the male and inserted into the female's vagina. It is used in cases where a natural mating is not possible. The AKC will register litters resulting from "A.I." breedings provided certain rules are followed: ". . . both the sire and the dam are present during the artificial mating, and provided that both the extraction and insemination are done by the same licensed veterinarian." The proper form, available from the AKC, must be completed and submitted with the litter registration application.

As an alternative, breeders can now have frozen or chilled fresh semen sent to them. This is an exciting innovation for dog breeders, but it is not without drawbacks. Artificial insemination has been used for years, but both animals must be present. This is still a very desirable breeding method as it prevents the transfer of diseases between dog and bitch.

The AKC approved the use of frozen semen in March, 1981. For an important stud dog, any number of semen vials can be frozen and offspring can be produced long after his death. In order to register a frozen semen litter, the semen must be stored at an AKC approved site. Thawing the frozen semen properly is critical. You should seek a veterinarian trained in the procedure if you are interested in this type of breeding.

In the fresh chilled semen process, the dog's ejaculate is collected, a buffer or extender solution is added and it is chilled. The semen is then shipped via express to the waiting bitch. Not every veterinarian is qualified to perform this service. It is expensive as both the collecting and administering veterinarians must be paid. In addition, the bitch's blood must be monitored almost daily to pinpoint the exact time of ovulation. There is a charge for the extender plus expenses for shipping. Some stud dog owners require that the semen be implanted directly into the bitch's uterus, which involves

surgery rather than vaginal insertion. With direct implantation, the successful conception rate is very high, but large litters have also been conceived without surgery which always entails some risk.

The use of either chilled or frozen semen presents great advantages to the breeder. A long dead dog or a dog from another country can sire a litter. Thus, the small gene pool in the United States can be enlarged, as can those in other countries. Genetic diversity is important as we try to eliminate Wheaten health problems.

After breeding, keep the bitch close to home. She is still capable of being bred, so make sure she is confined for at least another week. Try not to expose her to strange dogs. Never take a bred or pregnant bitch to a dog show.

How can you tell if your bitch is pregnant? You have to assume that she is, provided there were at least two successful matings. Your bitch may go off her food for a few weeks, but will become a voracious eater later in the pregnancy. She may vomit during the early weeks. My Kelly would just sleep. A sure sign of pregnancy was that Kelly refused cheese, a favorite treat.

THE GESTATION PERIOD

This is a time when your knowledge of your bitch's normal behavior comes in handy. It is not too difficult to spot unusual behavior patterns such as marked belching or increased need for sleep and affection. Experienced breeders can sometimes palpate fetal lumps during the fifth week, but it is difficult, especially with a young bitch who may carry her puppies high up.

I do not feel that x-rays should be used to determine pregnancy. If a bitch is pregnant, she's pregnant. If she isn't, you can't do any thing about it until her next season anyway. Even your veterinarian cannot always tell. With my first litter, in her eighth week, I dutifully took Kelly to the vet just to see if everything was okay. My vet said there were no puppies. She had either reabsorbed them or was having a false pregnancy. I was devastated. I completely ignored the fact that for several days I had been able to feel puppies moving when she was lying on her side. But if the vet said there were no puppies, he was the professional and he should know. Ten days later, she had eight lovely, healthy puppies and I changed veterinarians.

I learned three lessons from this harrowing experience. The first was that relatively few vets have had experience with normal whelpings. They get all the problems. The second was to trust my own knowledge and instincts. The third was that a vet who understands the serious breeder is a treasure.

Offer the bitch a nutritious, well-balanced diet (see section on diet) and observe her usual pattern of activity. The bitch knows best how much she wants to do. Avoid rough play during the last half of the pregnancy, but she will probably not want to be too active by then anyway. Also, if your bitch is quite heavy with puppies, she will most likely need to relieve herself more frequently.

Keep in mind that we are only hitting the highlights here. Consult one or more of the books on breeding that are listed in the Bibliography for more detailed information.

The gestation period is about sixty-three days, but may be over or under as much as three or four days. On about the fifty-seventh or fifty-eighth day from the first breeding, start taking your bitch's temperature in the morning and evening. When it begins to drop from its normal 101.5°, you know that whelping time is getting close. This drop in temperature helps lessen the shock to the newborn puppies when they come into a world that hovers at 85°. The bitch's temperature can go as low as 90°, but this is rare. A bitch may shiver at this time.

WHELPING

During the last week accustom your bitch to the place where you want her to whelp. If you have the available space, it is handy to have a fairly large whelping box that can serve until the puppies are ready to leave home. The one I used was four by four feet (see diagram). The box should have a shelf or rail so puppies cannot be easily crushed against the sides of the box. Line the bottom with heavy plastic and several layers of newspaper. After the whelping, you can line the box with unbacked indoor-outdoor carpet. Place it in a quiet area or in a separate room where the temperature can be raised to at least 85°. Have the following supplies at hand:

towels	clock
scale	alcohol
newspapers	blunt-nosed scissors
nail polish	Vaseline
heating pad	cotton balls
notepaper and pen	heater
thermometer	basket or box

Wheatens are usually free whelpers and generally take good care of their puppies. It is a rare bitch who is not a paragon of maternal virtue. Make sure your vet knows birth is imminent so he will be available if an emergency arises. As a rule, Wheatens have ample milk to feed their litters, but if the litter is large, and some puppies are not thriving, consult your vet about using supplementary food. Early weaning may make rearing the litter a bit easier on the bitch.

When birth is imminent, the bitch will pant heavily and contractions will be visible. She will probably scratch up the newspapers and bedding in the whelping box and will lick her outer genitalia in preparation for the birth of the litter. If your bitch strains without results for more than two hours, contact your vet.

In a normal whelping, the next thing that happens is that her water bag breaks. Soon afterward, a puppy in his sac appears. Be prepared to break the sac near the head so that the whelp can breathe. Let your bitch do as much as possible in attending to the puppy. The bitch should remove the sac and sever the umbilical cord. If she doesn't take the initiative, remove the sac and cut the cord about two inches from the puppy's body.

Most bitches will pitch right in, but if it is the bitch's first litter, she may not know what to do immediately. However, natural instincts soon take over, and the succeeding pups get the bitch's full attention. There is an afterbirth for each puppy and the bitch will consume them if permitted. I usually allow the bitch to eat two or three. Eating the afterbirths is Nature's way of providing a nutritious meal to a new mother. This also seems to stimulate additional contractions and help arouse maternal instincts. Every breeder has her own ideas about it. There is no wrong or right opinion on this point.

Place the newborn puppy at a nipple as soon as possible. This first milk (colostrum) provides immunity directly from the mother and is most important to a newborn's well-being. Nursing also stimulates uterine contractions. The bitch will lick the pup to dry it and stimulate it to breathe and eliminate. You can assist by gently rubbing the puppy with a rough towel. While the bitch is whelping additional pups, place the dry ones in a box or blanket lined with towels and a heating pad underneath. A chilled puppy is a dead puppy, so be sure to keep the room to at least 85° for the first week.

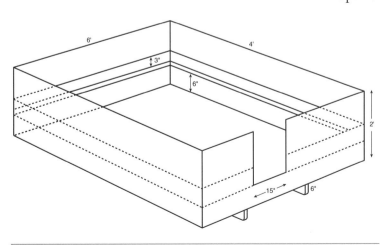

A schematic drawing of a typical whelping box showing the railing around the edges to protect the puppies.

A contented Wheaten mother soon after giving birth. Note that tails have not yet been docked. (photo by Sally Sotirovich)

Weigh each puppy right after it is delivered and mark it with nail polish. Mark each one in a different spot and record it in your notebook. This will give you an individual chart on each pup. For example: Male, left ear, twelve ounces, born at 5:10. The nail polish can be replaced if needed and it is safe. Some breeders use colored ribbon or rick rack collars. The object is to have a means of differentiating each puppy in order to keep a correct record of his progress. The chart will be a permanent record of the litter. If you continue breeding, those records of earlier litters become an invaluable point of reference.

When all the puppies have arrived, the bitch will rest comfortably, happily feeding her brood. Take her to the vet for a pituitrin or oxytocin shot within twenty-four to thirty-six hours. This causes contractions which helps to expel any retained afterbirths or placental residue. Make the appointment at the beginning of office hours and be early enough to avoid contact with other animals. Feed the bitch as much as she wants.

Your bitch has probably worked hard to present you with her litter and deserves special treatment. While the bitch is nursing, check the breasts and nipples frequently. If there is any sign of soreness or caking, consult your vet.

CARING FOR THE NEW PUPPIES

Wheatens have naturally long tails at birth that are normally docked at three days of age. About one third to one half the length of the tail is removed. It is better to err on the long side as it can be redone if necessary. The current trend is for a longer tail to balance the somewhat longer necks that seem to be occurring in today's Wheatens with greater regularity. In years past, short tails were the norm.

Your vet should know how to handle tail docking. It is relatively simple and nearly painless. But you will have specify where to cut. Hold the puppies up and measure the tail in relation to the neck, keeping in mind that in the adult, the tail should be one half to two thirds the length of the neck. When you decide on the length you want, clip the hair all around the tail at that point to provide a point of reference for your veterinarian.

Dewclaws are the vestigial remains of an extra toe. They are almost always present on the front feet where they are analogous the human thumb. Occasionally dewclaws appear on the rear legs, although I have never seen them or heard of anyone who has. If they are not removed, the nails grow long and the dog will chew at them. They can also be easily ripped during grooming or active play, causing the dog severe pain. Dewclaws serve no purpose in the Wheaten and having them removed in the neonate is the right course.

Most breeders start weaning their puppies after about four weeks. It is important to do this gradually so that the puppies' digestive tracts become used to a solid food diet. There is no hard and fast rule here. Each breeder has her own system and preference for handling this important part of a puppy's life.

I start my puppies on a fairly thin gruel made of one of the bitch's milk substitutes and baby rice cereal. It is warmed slightly and served in flat pie plates. I start with the midday meal and try to keep

A sight to warm any breeder's heart—a snuggling pile of plump Wheaten puppies. All the puppies wear color-coded rick-rack collars to facilitate their identification. (photo by Sally Sotirovich)

the dam away from the pups as much as possible during the day.

Once the pupppies are lapping well, I add some boiled chopped beef that has been whirled in the blender for a few seconds. I also increase the number of feedings to three times a day.

The next ingredient I add is ground puppy kibble and gradually remove the rice cereal. At least one meal contains cottage cheese, and I give the puppies scrambled eggs once or twice a week.

By the time they are six weeks old, the puppies are eating four solid food meals a day, and mama only visits to play and clean up the leftovers.

Your puppies must have a series of inoculations to give them immunity from certain preventable diseases. Different veterinarians use different methods. Some breeders give their own shots. Personally, I prefer to rely on my vet for this important part of puppy care.

You may be lucky enough to have a vet who will come to your home. If you do have to visit the office, try to get an appointment at the beginning or end of office hours so that contact with sick animals is minimized or avoided. Take the pups in when the vet is ready to see them. Keep a written record of the vaccines used and the date of inoculation.

PLACING THE PUPPIES

Placing your puppies is an activity that has the potential for disaster. It is the responsible breeder's most crucial decision. By the time the puppies are seven or eight weeks old, the breeder is eager to place them in good homes. This is the ideal age to place a puppy because bonding with the new family is easier, although many breeders want to hold them until they are twelve weeks old or more.

Evaluating potential owners is difficult. Some breeders will not sell a puppy to someone without a securely-fenced yard. Others do not want to place puppies in homes where everyone works, with some justification. Still others frown on Wheatens in city apartments. Some will not sell to a family without being assured the wife/mother truly wants a dog. This, too, is justified.

As a breeder, you want your puppies in the "perfect" home situation. You have put a great deal of time and effort into the litter and don't want your work to be undone by new owners who don't follow your detailed instructions. Take the time to get to know your prospects. Have them visit you and the pups several times. Observe how the parents deal with their own children. Undisciplined children often are an indication that the dog will also not be disciplined properly. Ask about the family's lifestyle and normal routines. Find out how much time the dog will spend alone. Here, as in many situations, common sense and intuition will go a long way in helping you select the right homes for the puppies you breed.

In placing puppies, always use a sales contract. Make sure as breeder, that you are able, willing and indeed, insistent on

Soft Coated Wheaten bitches make very attentive, devoted dams as this study in tenderness clearly depicts. (photo courtesy of Jana Carraway)

taking the dog back if the situation doesn't work out. There are cases where unscrupulous buyers obtain a bitch from a reputable breeder only to re-sell her to a puppy mill. Such people will probably go elsewhere rather than sign a strict contract or just ignore it if it is signed. Fortunately, such people are not common.

Having a contract with each buyer is more important than ever. You want to be sure that your puppy is not going to be resold without your knowledge. This is one way that Wheaten puppies end up in the wrong hands. The AKC has recently established a non-breeding "B" registration. Please contact their offices for detailed instructions for using it. This is one of the best weapons we have in the fight against irresponsible breeding. If breeders screen potential owners carefully, good placement will be the norm. The

While breeding dogs is definitely gratifying, it is equally exhausting. Here mom, breeder and puppies enjoy a well-deserved rest. (photo by Sally Sotirovich)

demand for Wheatens is fairly high at present. Breeders should consider pricing their dogs so that a family with an average income can afford one. High prices encourage people to breed to get their investment back. People do call the AKC to find out which breed is the most expensive so they can start a business based on that breed.

Breeders must also realize that not every dog is a potential champion. In Wheatens, even most of the champions are pets first and show dogs second. How fortunate is a breeder who takes a chance and places a quality puppy with a family, convinces them to show and encourages them to the point that they become active

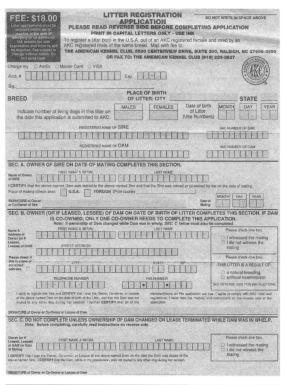

AKC Litter Registration Form.

exhibitors. The wise decisions of responsible breeders will determine where the Wheaten will stand in the dog world tomorrow and in the years ahead.

This chapter may seem to be a bit negative, but this is done with a purpose. If an owner is fully aware of the pitfalls and problems of breeding, he or she can make an intelligent decision about whether to breed or not. This is not meant to be a definitive discussion about breeding. There are numerous excellent books on the subject. Every breeder's library ought to have at least one or two. Consult the Bibliography in the Appendix section of this book for a listing of books on this important subject.

(photo © Close Encounters of the Furry Kind)

CHAPTER 13

Special Care for the Older Wheaten

In a society that worships youth, we do almost anything to ourselves to slow down the aging process. We exercise, diet, color our hair and try to replace it when and if it goes. Just as we recognize aging in ourselves, we have to be aware that our dogs are aging too.

LIFE EXPECTANCY

Wheatens generally live from ten to fifteen years, and for most of their lives they act like perennial puppies. Signs of aging just sort of creep up on us and our dogs. The gradual changes in your Wheaten's personality and activity level are hard to detect until one day you suddenly realize that his greeting is a bit less exuberant and that he sleeps more than he once did. On the other hand, your Wheaten may be more affectionate than he was in his youth.

Many people like to compare their dog's age to human years. One old standard was that each year of a dog's life was equal to seven years of a human's life. Common sense tells us that this system is less than accurate. In the first year of his life, a dog changes from an infant to a toddler to an adolescent to an adult. One formula counts this as twenty-one human years. After the first year, changes occur more slowly so rather than seven, this system adds four years for each year of a dog's life. The chart below is based on this formula.

Dog's Age	Human's Age
1	21
2	25
3	29
4	33
5	37
6	41
7	45
8	49
9	53
10	57
11	61
12	65
13	69
14	73
15	77
16	81
17	85
18	89
19	93
20	97

While this may be a more realistic approach, it merely provides guidelines and should not be thought of as scientific fact. Different breeds do age at different rates and even individuals within a breed show variation in longevity. The important thing is to be aware of the subtle changes in your dog's personality, activity level and appearance. Let us look more closely at these occurrences.

EXERCISE AND DIET

It is assumed that your Wheaten has been fed optimally and exercised and groomed regularly since it was a puppy. The older dog needs fewer calories

Two senior citizens, "Misty" (Ch. Clanheath's Misty Clover, ROM) (at left) at age ten and "Jody" (Ch. Andover Lucky Treasure, CD) at eleven. (photo by Bryan McNamara)

than a young, active animal. He needs less protein, but it must be of high quality. Fresh water should always be available. There are foods formulated for older dogs and you may wish to explore this area with your veterinarian and your dog's breeder. In my experience, the signs of old age are not noticeable until well after ten years. Even those are not always serious or debilitating. What should we be looking for?

The older dog will be less active, but with a Wheaten less does not necessarily mean sedentary. My first dog lived to be almost sixteen. She still wanted her walks even though she moved more slowly. Your older dog will probably sleep a great deal more than he did when he was younger. It is vital that you see to it that your dog still gets the right amount of exercise. Long, leisurely walks are ideal for the aging Wheaten.

Your dog's body systems will slow down. If incontinence should become a problem, your veterinarian should be consulted, as a variety of treatments are available. Obviously, your dog will need more opportunities to relieve him/herself. This condition tends to be more common in bitches.

Am., Can. Ch. Desert Sun's Abbey Chermar, CD at age fourteen enjoying a soft, comfortable spot. (photo by Sally Sotirovich)

HEALTH CONCERNS

Your Wheaten may become constipated. If this happens, try to give your dog fresh raw vegetables in his food. If it becomes really serious, consult your veterinarian. If you are not already using an enzyme supplement, this may be a good time to begin. These products enhance your dog's natural digestive process by adding digestive enzymes that cooked foods lack. Yogurt may also be given if it contains live cultures.

Grooming your older Wheaten is as necessary as ever, perhaps even more so. This is the time you look for lumps and bumps. Check the skin for signs of dryness or inflammation. The coat will also tend to thin out as the dog ages. You will probably want to keep his coat trimmed fairly short so that there is less hair to comb, which will shorten the grooming time and limit the potential for creating unnecessary stress. You could also do it more frequently in brief sessions. Also, don't neglect your dog's nails.

Check your dog's eyes regularly for signs of irritation. You may notice the cloudiness that comes with cataracts. Cataracts are fairly common, but they may be associated with diabetes, which can be revealed by a blood test.

Teeth can cause problems in the older dog as well as the younger animal. A build-up of tartar causes other infections that can affect the liver and kidneys and cause bad breath. Continue with your dog's regular dental care program. Currently veterinarians are paying more attention to preventive care. They are becoming more aware of how periodontal disease can affect other parts of the body. If your dog has a heavy build-up of tartar and thick, reddened gums that bleed easily, see your veterinarian.

Assuming you have properly cared for your dog throughout his life and provided a nutritious diet with regular exercise and grooming, your dog's golden years can be a wonderful time for the whole family. Your dog will especially welcome extra attention and quiet time at this stage of his life.

Accidents are the most frequent cause of death in dogs. Diseases like cancer, heart problems and deteriorating kidney function all occur in dogs. There are no hard statistics on how frequently these conditions occur in Wheatens.

WHEN THE END COMES

The inevitable death of one's beloved Wheaten is the hardest thing to contemplate. The time will come when your dog may be in serious pain.

Perhaps he has to be helped to walk. It is entirely up to you as to when you think the dog's quality of life has deteriorated to the extent that it would be better if he were beyond his pain. It would be wonderful if our dogs just died peacefully in their sleep. Realistically, it just doesn't work that way. When my first Wheaten was being treated for congestive heart failure, I used to almost hope that she would die while I was away at work. She was taking a diuretic and had to be confined to the kitchen. I finally realized that losing her "ruler of the roost" status with free rein had made her life miserable. My husband and I made arrangements with the vet and the crematory. We were with her to the end and we both cried as she died in our arms. We had almost sixteen years of unconditional love from Kelly. As hard as it was, euthanasia was the right thing to do for her and for our family at the time.

There are other things to consider when your dog dies. If it happens at home, disposal of the body becomes a consideration. It may be unpleasant, but planning is important especially if you want to use a pet cemetery. Communities have laws regarding pet burial so home burial may not be an option. Formal burial is the most expensive method. Cremation is more common and your vet can help you make arrangements. If you wish to have your dog's remains returned to you it will be necessary to pay for a more costly individual cremation rather than a collective one.

It is not abnormal or crazy to grieve for an animal. It is perfectly natural to feel a void when your faithful friend is no longer with you. If you feel the need for additional consolation, there are helpful books and support groups available. One of the best ways to ease the pain of loss is to consider a new puppy. Again, this is a personal decision. I know it helped me to have Kelly's daughter around at that difficult time.

(photo © Close Encounters of the Furry Kind)

The Soft Coated Wheaten Terrier Club of America

Breed clubs are formed to preserve, protect and promote a particular breed of dog. Typically, these clubs are formed when a group of fanciers becomes acquainted and decides to organize. They contact other known owners and solicit members. They write a constitution and by-laws. If there is no breed Standard, they write one. The members hold meetings and conduct other kinds of events to stimulate interest in the breed and thereby achieve their goals.

During the early years of the American Kennel Club, it was simple for a club to become a member. One just applied. Now there is a set procedure that requires a number of steps through various levels toward full membership. In the case of a single-breed club, if the breed is still in the Miscellaneous Class, sanction is not possible until the breed is accepted into the Stud Book.

Acceptance into the Miscellaneous Class is the first step toward AKC recognition for a breed striving to achieve that goal. A national club for a Miscellaneous breed can only hold "fun" matches. These events must be held in various parts of the country. The club also must keep accurate records of dogs and breedings, including import pedigrees. Wide geographic distribution of dogs is a must.

THE EARLY YEARS

In 1947 when Wheaten fancier Lydia Vogel marched into the AKC offices with her Wheaten pedigrees and photos, she had no idea what AKC requirements for recognition were. In fact, in 1947, the Miscellaneous Class as it is known today did not exist. There was no list of eligible breeds. Any breed for which a show did not offer regular classification had to be shown in the Miscellaneous Class. There was even a time when these dogs were eligible for further competition. It was no wonder Lydia was disheartened by the AKC's response of January 3, 1947, a portion of which is quoted here:

Our rules for recognition of a new breed of purebred dogs requires, among other things, applications for at least 25 dogs of a breed, the formation of a club for the purpose of forwarding the interests of the breed, a breed Standard, etc. . . .

Lydia sent a letter stating that there was a club. She even submitted a set of by-laws. For numerous reasons, Lydia Vogel's efforts were unfruitful. Perhaps she was so over extended she was not free to devote herself solely to this goal. She bred and showed Kerry Blues, was a professional handler and had a grooming business.

Margaret O'Connor, however, had the energy and the desire to gain AKC recognition for the Wheaten. Since a club was needed, she started one. On St. Patrick's Day in 1962 a group of Wheaten owners and three Wheatens met in the Brooklyn (New York) home of Professor Louis and Ida Mallory. The result was the formation of the Soft Coated Wheaten Terrier Club of America (SCWTCA). The first officers were:

President:	Margaret O'Connor
Vice President:	Ida Mallory
Secretary:	Eileen Jackson

The Club's initial action was to send out a newsletter. It was called *Wheaten Wires* and went to twenty-five SCWT owners and supporters. By July, Margaret realized that the title was inappropriate for a soft coated dog, so the name was changed to *Benchmarks* and is still published quarterly under that name.

When she chose the new name, Margaret explained that "A benchmark, according to Webster, is a point of reference from which measurements of any sort may be made. Since we hope to measure the growth and popularity of the Soft Coated Wheaten Terrier through this publication, we feel *Benchmarks* to be the appropriate name."

The following year, Margaret's sister, Eileen Jackson was elected as SCWTCA's Secretary/Treasurer, an indication that there were club funds. There were so few members at this time that all efforts centered on locating more Wheaten owners. Margaret submitted articles to the major dog magazines, but since Wheatens were only in the Miscellaneous class, they did not make "hot copy." Still, Margaret persevered and had some success, notably her column for *Terrier Type*. Little emphasis was placed on formal meetings or by-laws in this developmental period.

The Club concentrated on two activities, maintaining the Stud Book and publishing

Benchmarks. It published a small booklet about Wheatens and distributed it to interested people. The basic problem was that there simply were not enough dogs and owners to really have an active club. There was no mention of holding a Specialty match or more formal show.

In 1963, when Margaret O'Connor wrote her first column in *Terrier Type,* she stated proudly "there are now twenty-nine Wheatens known to be in the United States." Given the level of individual interest and the wide geographic dispersal of owners, it is understandable that the business of the Club revolved around the O'Connors and a few friends who lived close to New York City.

GROWTH AND MATURITY

But times were changing. A year after Margaret O'Connor's death in 1968, there were close to 250 Wheatens registered in the Club's records. This statistic translated to more club members since breeders at the time encouraged new owners to register their dogs and join the Club.

A major factor leading to increased Club activity was the extensive breeding done by the Charles Arnolds and a few others. As people purchased dogs, they registered them with the Soft Coated Wheaten Terrier Club of America and joined the Club. It was only a matter of time before someone would suggest holding a match.

Dog clubs lend themselves to contention without special effort. There always seem to be factions, even in clubs of long standing and great stability. The Wheaten fancy was and is no different. A small

but influential group was dissatisfied with the way the Club was progressing toward AKC recognition. Rightly or wrongly, this group aimed a certain amount of criticism at the O'Connors.

This "rebel" group recognized that there had to be Specialty matches. As these pioneer Wheaten exhibitors showed their dogs, they were exposed to exhibitors of other Miscellaneous Class breeds such as the Shih Tzu who had gained AKC status while the Wheaten remained in limbo. The "graduated" Shih Tzu fanciers informed Wheaten people how important matches were. Inevitably, the die was cast.

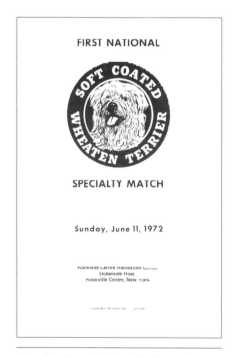

FIRST NATIONAL

SOFT COATED WHEATEN TERRIER

SPECIALTY MATCH

Sunday, June 11, 1972

Rockville Centre Recreation Center
Oceanside Road
Rockville Centre, New York

Catalog from the first "fun" match sponsored by the SCWTCA.

THE FIRST MATCH SHOWS

On March 22, 1970 a Wheaten "fun match" was held in Rockville Centre, New York. There were thirty-five entries and Best in Match went to Leprecaun's Top Shoemaker (Gramachree's Minute Man, CDX ex Maretthay`s Irish Colleen) owned by Peter and Judy Siegel of Rockville Centre. John Cox was the judge.

The second fun match was held on June 6, 1971, again at Rockville Centre. It was hosted by the newly formed Soft Coated Wheaten Terrier Club of Metropolitan New York. Clark Thompson judged the entry of fifty-two Wheatens. The future champion Stephen Dedalus of Andover, CD was Best in Match.

With the election of new officers for 1970, there was a significant change in the Club's management. The O'Connors were no longer strongly represented on the Board of Directors. In the Winter 1969 issue of *Benchmarks*, Mrs. Cecelia O'Connor and Eileen Jackson gave their final reports as President and Secretary, respectively. Cecelia continued as editor of *Benchmarks* until 1973.

By opening the Board to new participants from a wider spectrum, the Club took another step toward fuller participation in the sport and moved closer to AKC recognition. In the process, the ongoing conflict about the coat and trimming surfaced again and again.

Though the Club was founded in 1962, a constitution was not approved by the membership until 1968. A meeting held in November 1969 failed to bring in a sufficient number for a quorum, so no actions were taken. It turned out to be just an informal gathering with some heated discussion about the progress of the breed and the Club.

Without the O'Connor family the Soft Coated Wheaten Terrier's progress might have taken much longer. Their dedication produced the set of vital records that AKC required. Margaret, and later her mother, maintained communication with Wheaten owners and SCWTCA members during the Club's formative years. They encouraged others to show and offered trophies for Wheatens who won Obedience titles. In Eileen Jackson's last report as Secretary, she quotes Casey Stengel talking about the 1969 New York Mets World Series victory. He said "They came along fast but slow." What an appropriate statement!

CONTROVERSY AND CONTENTION

The years 1970 to 1973 were years of rapid movement toward recognition by the AKC. More people were showing their dogs. The Soft Coated Wheaten Terrier Club of America was giving Specialty matches. There was beginning to be some uniformity of presentation. However, there were differences of opinion as to what constituted "tidying" and just what was meant by a "neat outline." Wheatens were being shown both in full coat and trimmed.

In 1971, a group calling itself the Breeder-Exhibitor Education Society placed ads in the major dog magazines and mailed information to Wheaten owners and anyone else who contacted them. The SCWTCA then placed advertisements in those same magazines setting forth its own credentials as the national breed club. The "BEES" buzzed around for awhile but its members eventually began to work through the Soft Coated Wheaten Terrier Club of America toward AKC recognition.

At the time, the differences of opinion regarding coat presentation created a major issue among fanciers. Battle lines were drawn. It was trimmers vs. non-trimmers. It is interesting to note that there is no longer any conflict about whether to trim or not. The question today is how and how much.

Another issue that came before the SCWTCA Board was the idea of constitutional revision. It was never possible to have a quorum. The by-laws just were not adequate for a national breed club. Charles Arnold was largely responsible for suggesting changes. Most of his proposals were denied at first but later the revisions he suggested went into effect. The Club revised the constitution and by-laws and brought them more into line with AKC requirements in 1973 as a prerequisite for recognition.

Another somewhat minor controversy surrounded breed classification. There was a rather vocal group who wanted the breed to go into the Non-Sporting or Working Group. As history shows, they were not successful.

Great credit must be given to the Board of Directors for maintaining a collective cool head during those crucial years 1971 to 1972. The Club did not fall apart in spite of internal squabbling. In October 1972, President Tom O'Connor received notification from the AKC that it was likely that the SCWTCA Stud Book might be accepted early in 1973. Reporting about an informal membership meeting in November 1972, Cecelia O'Connor expressed chagrin that little appreciation was shown for the efforts made by past members toward acceptance.

OFFICIAL AKC RECOGNITION

Now that the recognition was at hand, instead of celebrating, the Wheaten fancy continued to argue about trimming and control of the Club. However, in spite of the conflicts, the goal was reached on March 13, 1973, when AKC approved the addition of the Soft Coated Wheaten Terrier to the Terrier Group. Show eligibility was set for October 1, 1973.

The next goal for the Club was to become eligible to hold AKC events. That approval came fairly quickly. The first Sanctioned Plan B Match was held on November 11, 1973, in Macungie, Pennsylvania, and the second on June 15, 1974, in Livingston, New Jersey. On September 21, 1974, SCWTCA held its first required Plan A sanctioned match in Merion, Pennsylvania. The second A match was held on April 13, 1975, in Rockville Centre, New York. The Soft Coated Wheaten Terrier Club of America had now completed all AKC match requirements and was eligible to apply for permission to hold licensed events, that is, shows at which points toward championships can be awarded.

CLUB ACTIVITIES

SCWTCA held its first Specialty show in conjunction with the prestigious Montgomery County Kennel Club all-terrier show on October 5, 1975. Ch. Raclee's Express West O'Andover (Ch. Glenworth's Country Squire ROM ex Ch. Raclee's Serendipity) was Best of Breed. Best of Opposite

Sex was Ch. Raclee's Extra Special, a littermate to the Best of Breed. A complete list of SCWTCA Specialty winners appears in Appendix E.

Holding a Specialty became the major event of the Club's year, but there was other business to be accomplished. In 1973 the format of *Benchmarks* underwent a significant change. The publication had been printed on regular paper and had no illustrations. In its new format, *Benchmarks* looked like a real magazine. Marjorie Shoemaker was appointed editor, a position she held for the next ten years.

That same year, the Soft Coated Wheaten Terrier Club of America started its breed referral service. The service aimed to put people in contact with reliable member-breeders as sources for puppies. The Board appointed a Standard revision committee headed by Gay Sherman (Dunlap).

In 1975, Jackie Gottlieb and Cindy Vogels undertook the publication of a newsletter, *Wavelengths*, designed to communicate timely information and official Club actions to the membership.

The Breeder Referral Service became the Breeder Information Service. The "Shake Hands" brochure was introduced. The Club aimed to generate more information about Wheatens so that it would be easier for potential owners to decide if the Wheaten was really what they wanted. Currently, SCWTCA distributes a "Buyer's Guide" that replaces that earlier brochure. Work also began on a Code of Ethics, and the Soft Coated Wheaten Terrier Owner's Manual.

In 1976, SCWTCA held its first roving Specialty in Colorado. That same year, the Board appointed Jackie Gottlieb as the regular breed columnist for the *AKC Gazette*, a position she still holds.

BENCHMARKS

PUBLISHED QUARTERLY BY THE SOFT COATED WHEATEN TERRIER CLUB OF AMERICA, INC.
Volume 1, Number 1   FALL 1973

featuring:

- **The Top Ten Wheatens**
- **Article by John T. Marvin**
  noted judge and writer
- **Grooming for the Show Ring**

The cover of the Fall 1973 issue of Benchmarks *was the first in its current format.*

The first few years saw SCWTCA grow in stature and activity. The Club became involved in investigating and supporting research on genetic defects. "The Soft Coated Wheaten Terrier Owner's Manual" became a reality in 1979. Revised editions were made in 1984 and 1994. A new Standard was approved in February, 1982. SCWTCA started an eye registry and instituted the policy that breeding stock had to be OFA (Orthopedic Foundation for Animals) certified before owners could be included on the approved breeders list.

The Board of Directors approved a club logo, designed by Marjorie Shoemaker with Gay Sherman's (now Dunlap) help in 1978. The logo appears on Club stationery and publications as well as trophies. It is cast in a pewter medallion, which is given to any member whose dog becomes a champion.

The SCWTCA is dedicated to helping people locate sound, healthy Soft Coated Wheaten Terriers from reputable breeders who subscribe to the Club's stringent Code of Ethics. As part of this program, when Wheatens are found in any undesirable channels of supply, the Club underwrites the cost of placing a Club advertisement in the local newspaper. This activity is coordinated with local clubs.

The American Kennel Club has high expectations for dog clubs holding events under its rules. Maintaining these standards is particularly crucial for parent Specialty clubs. Becoming an AKC member club takes time and effort. A club must have acceptable by-laws and must demonstrate a knowledge of AKC rules and policies. Its membership must have a strong core of breeders and exhibitors. A Specialty club is expected to educate the public and its members through articles in magazines, books and pamphlets. Perhaps the most significant task is that of keeper of the breed Standard.

AKC MEMBERSHIP

AKC's Board of Directors accepted the application of the SCWTCA to become a member club on September 13, 1983. Gay Sherman (now Dunlap) was appointed as the first AKC delegate. The Soft Coated Wheaten Terrier Club of America continues to function as the official voice in all matters regarding the breed. It holds an annual Specialty and usually sponsors a roving Specialty, often every other year.

The SCWTCA publishes two periodicals, *Benchmarks*, its quarterly magazine, and *Wavelengths*. Anyone can subscribe to *Benchmarks*, but *Wavelengths* is only sent to Club members. It reports the official actions of the Board of Directors and committees, gives Specialty show results and provides other timely information.

The Club also publishes *The Soft Coated Wheaten Terrier Yearbook*. This publication is a continuation of the "green book," a hardcover volume entitled *SCWTCA Celebrating Ten Years of Recognition, 1973–1982*, compiled under the editorship of Cindy Vogels, a long time breeder-exhibitor and AKC approved judge. It lists all champions and Obedience title holders with their pedigrees as well as results of Wheaten Specialty shows and Club awards. The first volume includes pedigrees of the early imports and some Irish foundation stock. It is an invaluable source for pedigree research and for studying photographs of nearly every Wheaten champion. Now published annually, this yearbook is an excellent resource for all Wheaten breeders and for anyone who wants to see how any Wheaten champion's ancestors looked.

In 1992 the Club published an illustrated Standard and amplification as an aid to breeders and judges. It was edited by Gay Dunlap and designed and illustrated by Jody Sylvester. Ms.

*The SCWTCA's current public informa-
tion booklet, The Soft Coated Wheaten
Terrier—A Buyer's Guide.*

*The Soft Coated Wheaten Terrier
Owner's Manual.*

Dunlap is one of the stalwarts in the breed who is also an AKC approved judge.

The Club distributes "The Soft Coated Wheaten Terrier, A Buyer's Guide" to anyone who requests information about the breed. It describes the Wheaten and tells prospective buyers how to find and evaluate breeders. It also includes an order form for Club publications.

Through its various committees and publications, SCWTCA continues to fulfill its role as protector of the breed. Club members generously support the rescue programs and health research.

The AKC Canine Health Foundation awarded Dr. Shelly Vaden of North Carolina State College of Veterinary Medicine a three year grant to study protein losing enteropathy (PLE) and protein losing nephropathy (PLN) in Wheatens. SCWTCA members donated 174 percent of the required matching funds. The Club maintains close ties to the Soft Coated Wheaten Terrier Club of Canada and to British and European fanciers and underwrote an international conference in October 1998 in conjunction with its Specialty show.

Epilogue

When I wrote *The Complete Soft Coated Wheaten Terrier* I was totally committed to the project. While that same dedication continues with this new book, it is now shared, to a great extent, by two grandchildren, my new-found love for quilting and major changes in my lifestyle.

During this project I learned that there is still work to be done in the Wheaten world. The breed's health problems are now being openly discussed rather than whispered about. The Wheaten fancy has even gone global. Thanks to the Internet, breeders all over the world can contact each other and discuss dogs quickly and conveniently, even if old timers like me approach it with a dose of technophobia. Reliable information is available almost instantly via the Internet.

There are new breeders coming along. They are fortunate that in the Soft Coated Wheaten Terrier fancy, they have so many mentors to consult. The SCWTCA is a strong, viable breed club. Whenever I see so many unfamiliar kennel names in the catalog ads for our annual national Specialty at the Montgomery County KC all-terrier show, I realize that the Wheaten world is no longer the small fraternity it once was. I hope the newcomers take advantage of the knowledge available to them and build on it. If they keep the betterment of the breed first and foremost in their minds, then there is great reason to be optimistic about the Wheaten's future.

Resources List

The following list contains the names and addresses of several organizations that may be of interest to Soft Coated Wheaten Terrier owners. Be aware, however, that addresses are subject to change. The American Kennel Club and the American Kennel Club Library are the ultimate source for the most current information. The names of local Soft Coated Wheaten Terrier Clubs and the names and addresses of their current secretaries are available from the secretary of the Soft Coated Wheaten Terrier Club of America, whose name is available from the American Kennel Club.

ORGANIZATIONS

AKC *Gazette* Editorial Offices
260 Madison Avenue
New York, NY 10017
212-696-8390

American Kennel Club
5580 Centerview Drive
Suite 200
Raleigh, NC 27606-3390
919-233-9767
www.akc.org

American Kennel Club Library
260 Madison Avenue
New York, NY 10017
212-696-8245

American Kennel Club Museum of the Dog
Jarville House
1721 Mason Road
St. Louis, MO 63131
314-821-3647

American Veterinary Medical Association (AVMA)
1931 N. Meacham Road #100
Schaumburg, IL 60173-4360

American Working Terrier Association (AWTA)
Cindy Todd, Treasurer
6861 Greenleaf Drive
N. Richland Hills, TX 76180
817-485-1075
Email: ctodd@juno.com

Canine Eye Registry Foundation (CERF)
c/o Alan Warble, Vet Med Data Program
South Campus Courts Building C
Purdue University
West Lafayette, IN 47907
317-494-8179
Fax: 317-494-9982

Orthopedic Foundation for Animals (OFA)
Dr. D.A. Corley
2300 E. Nifong Boulevard
Columbia, MO 62501-3856

PennHip
Symbiotic Corp.
11011 Via Frontera
San Diego, CA 92127

Therapy Dogs International
6 Hilltop Road
Mendham, NJ 07945
201-543-0888

GROOMING VIDEOS

Practically Perfect Pets ($31.95 + $2.50 S&H)
Department WD
PO Box 41565
Plymouth, MN 55441
612-347-0558

Video Clips ($39.95)
28830 Bison Court
Malibu, CA 90265

Code of Ethics: Soft Coated Wheaten Terrier Club of America, Inc.

The Code of Ethics is presented to all members of the SCWTCA, Inc. whose foremost objectives are the welfare, improvement and advancement of the breed in accordance with the Standard. This Code outlines basic procedure and sets forth principles of general conduct to be followed by all Club members.

1. General Conduct

   A. Each member will consider the welfare of the breed when engaged in breeding, exhibiting or selling Soft Coated Wheaten Terriers and will refrain from actions which are contrary to the best interests of the breed and the Club.

   B. Every dog shall be provided with humane living quarters, veterinarian supervised health care, proper nutrition and grooming.

C. Each member will be familiar with and abide by the rules and regulations of the American Kennel Club regarding the registering and exhibiting of Soft Coated Wheaten Terriers and the keeping of accurate records of breeding and exhibiting.

D. Good sportsmanship will be exhibited at all times.

E. Each Club member will be responsible at all times for the behavior of his dogs, such behavior to reflect the best possible image of the Soft Coated Wheaten Terrier.

F. All members will promote the cause of responsible dog ownership.

2. Breeding Soft Coated Wheaten Terriers

A. Only AKC registered dogs will be bred.

B. Breeders will aim to produce sound, healthy, happy dogs true to breed characteristics as set forth in the breed Standard of the Soft Coated Wheaten Terrier.

C. All breeding stock must be of sound temperament and possess no major hereditary defects. They must be in good health, free of parasites and communicable diseases, e.g. brucellosis, genital infections, etc. Testing for these will be done as close to breeding time as possible.

D. All breeding stock over two years of age will be OFA certified. All breeding stock under two years of age will be x-rayed and show no clinical signs of hip dysplasia.

E. All breeding stock will have eyes examined at least every two years by a Board Certified Veterinary Ophthalmologist. This will be done until at least six years of age. It is recommended that dogs and bitches being used extensively for breeding continue beyond the age of six.

F. Only mature dogs and bitches will be used for breeding.

1. A bitch will not be bred on her first season and preferably not before her third season or 18 months of age. In the event that the bitch is bred on two successive seasons or twelve months, that bitch will not be bred during the next two successive seasons or twelve months.

2. Dogs should not be used at stud before 11 months of age and should have preliminary OFA certification or OFA number. Written stud contracts will be used for each breeding.

3. Selling Soft Coated Wheaten Terriers

A. No dogs will knowingly be sold to pet dealers, pet wholesalers, or pet brokers, singly or in "litter lots."

B. Soft Coated Wheaten Terriers will not be offered as raffle or contest prizes or for other types of give-aways.

C. All advertising describing kennels and dogs offered for sale will be of an honest and forthright nature.

D. The breeder will provide AKC registration papers, application forms and/or other written contract if registration papers are to be withheld at the time of sale or within 30 days following delivery. It is recommended that the contract include a stipulation whereby the breeder be notified of any plan on the part of the owner to resell or otherwise dispose of a pup. This stipulation would also require the buyer to either return the dog to the breeder or place the dog with new owners who have been approved by the breeder. Breeder will also require buyer to advise of any health problems, physical abnormalities and/or the death of the animal. All conditions of sale agreed upon by the buyer and breeder must be in writing; when a non-registration or non-breeding clause is included a copy of the contract should be sent to the AKC. All animals sold as pets will be sold on spay/neuter agreement, and/or AKC limited registration.

E. All Soft Coated Wheaten Terriers will be in good condition and good health at the time of delivery. The dog/puppy, to the best of the seller's knowledge, will be free of internal parasites and will have protection against those diseases which can be controlled by vaccination according to current veterinary practices. At the time of delivery the seller will furnish medical records indicating the date of vaccination and the medication used.

F. An accurate pedigree of at least four generations as well as complete written instructions on feeding, health care, training and grooming of the dog/puppy will be furnished at the time of sale.

4. Exhibiting Soft Coated Wheaten Terriers

A. AKC rules concerning entering shows and exhibiting dogs will be strictly observed.

B. Dogs will be presented in the show ring clean and properly groomed according to the Standard. Any change of appearance by artificial means other than docking tails and removing dew claws (in accordance with the Standard) is strictly forbidden.

C. Exhibitors will conduct themselves in a sportsmanlike manner in and out of the ring.

D. The owner of record will be responsible for appearance and conduct of his dog at all times.

5. Discipline

A. Failure to comply with the Code of Ethics will subject a member to disciplinary procedures provided by the Constitution and By-Laws of the SCWTCA, Inc.

B. Allegation of violation of the Code of Ethics shall be adjudicated by the Board of Directors of the SCWTCA, Inc.

Available Titles, SCWTCA Awards and Key to Award Abbreviations

AKC CHAMPIONSHIP TITLES (ALWAYS PRECEDE DOG'S NAME)

Ch.—Conformation champion
OTCH—Obedience Trial champion

AKC OBEDIENCE TITLES (ALWAYS FOLLOW DOG'S NAME)

CD—Companion Dog

CDX—Companion Dog Excellent

UD—Utility Dog

UDX—Utility Dog Excellent

AKC TRACKING TITLES
(ALWAYS FOLLOW DOG'S NAME)

TD—Tracking Dog

TDX—Tracking Dog Excellent

VST—Variable Surface Tracking Test

CT—Champion Tracker

AKC AGILITY TITLES
(ALWAYS FOLLOW DOG'S NAME)

NA—Novice Agility

OA—Open Agility

AX—Agility Excellent

MX—Master Agility Excellent

SPECIAL TITLES

CGC—Canine Good Citizen (administered by AKC)

Dogs can attain Therapy Dog status through several Therapy Dog organizations.

SCWTCA AWARDS

The following awards are offered through the Soft Coated Wheaten Terrier Club of America. Complete details of each can be had from the secretary.

Register of Merit (ROM)—For sires of at least 15 champions or dams of at least 8 champions

Best in Show Award—For winners of an AKC all-breed Best in Show

Ch. Abby's Postage Dhu O' Waterford "Casey" Award

Amaden Award

Andover Challenge

Julian B. Turner Memorial

Ch. Gleanngay Holliday "Doc" Award

Everett Keller Memorial Trophy

Maureen Holmes Memorial Trophy

Brian E. McNamara Memorial Trophy

Harry and Betty Blair Memorial

Jan Linscheid Fellowship

High in Trial Award—For winners of a High in Trial at any AKC dog show or Obedience Trial (not a SCWT Specialty)

Obedience Dog of the Year

Junior Showmanship

SCWTCA Rescue Family of the Year

AWARD ABBREVIATIONS

WD—Winners Dog

RWD—Reserve Winners Dog

WB—Winners Bitch

RWB—Reserve Winners Bitch

BW—Best of Winners

BB—Best of Breed

BOS—Best of Opposite Sex

Gr. 1—Group 1st (Subsequent Group placements are expressed Gr. 2, Gr. 3 and Gr. 4)

BIS—Best in Show

BISS—Best in Specialty Show

AOM—Award of Merit

BPG—Best Puppy in Group

BPS—Best Puppy in Show

HIT—High in Trial

Soft Coated Wheaten Terrier Health Protocols

HEALTH ISSUES

Chair: George Jeitles, DVM
Coordinator: Elizabeth Ampleford
Committee Members:

Ilze Barron
Dr. Wendy Beers
Carol Carlson
Ronnie Copland
Jackie Gottleib
Beth Heckermann

Ann Holahan
Emily Holden
Richard Tomlinson

The Health Issues Committee of the SCWTCA receives and coordinates information regarding health problems within the breed. Research on protein-losing diseases and renal dysplasia is being conducted by the following veterinarians:

Dr. Shelly Vaden (Renal Diseases/Protein-losing Enteropathy)
College of Veterinary Medicine
North Carolina State University
4700 Hillsborough Street
Raleigh, NC 27606
919-829-4200
vaden@sn1.cvm.ncsu.edu

Dr. Meryl Littman (Renal Diseases/Protein-losing Enteropathy)
School of Veterinary Medicine, University of Pennsylvania

3900 Delancey Street, Philadelphia, PA 19104-6010
215-898-9288
fax 215-573-6050
merylitt@vet.upenn.edu

Dr. Brian Wilcock (Tissue Biopsies)
Ontario Veterinary College, University of Guelph
Guelph, Ontario, Canada N1G 2W1
519-824-4120 ext. 4655
(These veterinarians should not be contacted directly, but through one's own veterinarian. Medical data and pedigrees of affected dogs should be sent to Dr. Littman.)

RECOMMENDED PROTOCOL FOR PROTEIN-LOSING NEPHROPATHY/ENTEROPATHY SCREENING

Clinical Signs of PLN

PLN is difficult to diagnose, and the initial stages of the disease may be mistaken for liver, glandular or other enteric or kidney diseases. An abnormality on the glomeruli usually causes PLN. Some of the common signs and symptoms are:

Listlessness/depression

Decreased appetite, vomiting, weight loss

Ascites, edema, pleural effusion

Increased water consumption, increased urination (less common)

Thromboembolic phenomena and hypertension (less common)

Laboratory Abnormalities Associated with PLN

Hypoalbuminemia

Elevated serum creatinine, BUN

Hypercholesterolemia

Elevated urine protein/creatinine ratio

Clinical Signs of PLE

PLE is usually caused by lymphangiestacia or inflammatory bowel disease. In affected Wheatens there is a stimulation of the immune system in the bowel wall. Some of the common signs and symptoms are:

Vomiting

Diarrhea

Weight loss

Ascites

Edema

Pleural effusion

Laboratory Abnormalities Associated with PLE

Hypoalbuminemia

Hypoglobulinemia

Eosinophilia

Hypocholesterolemia

Lymphopenia

Screening Tests for PLN/PLE

Biochemical profile (often called chem screen or vet screen). This must include:

Total protein, albumin, creatinine and cholesterol

Complete blood count (optional)

Routine urinalysis (specific gravity, dipstick urinary sediment)

Urine protein/creatinine ratio

Fecal API

CLINICAL SIGNS OF RENAL DYSPLASIA

Increased water consumption, increased urination (dilute urine)

Poor doer, decreased appetite, vomiting

Possibly prone to urinary tract infection

Laboratory and Radiographic Abnormalities Associated with RD

Low urine specific gravity

Elevated creatinine and BUN

Small kidneys

Screening Tests for RD

Urinalysis, chem screen

Abdominal radiographs/ultrasound

Kidney biopsy (wedge, not Tru-cut); call Dr. Littman to discuss size

If these test results show any abnormalities, the client's veterinarian should contact Dr. Littman or Dr. Vaden for further advice.

PROTOCOL FOR POST-MORTEM EXAMINATIONS OF SOFT COATED WHEATEN TERRIERS WITH SUSPECTED PROTEIN-LOSING ENTEROPATHY/NEPHROPATHY OR RENAL DYSPLASIA

Before the dog is euthanized, the veterinarian calls Dr. Littman to discuss the case and help decide whether other samples (e.g. frozen kidneys) should be submitted or if test results are sufficient.

If the dog is deceased, the veterinarian follows these procedures:

1. After thorough examination of all organs, collect the following samples as stated so that each tissue can be readily identified.

   Kidneys: cut in halves longitudinally; submit in entirety in formalin. Note: for puppies with suspected renal dysplasia, only kidneys need to be submitted.

   Jejunum, ilium, cecum, colon: submit section which contains all four tissues as found in situ.

   Duodenum: submit with section of pancreas attached.

2. For adequate fixation, place samples of volume in formalin that approximates 10–20 times the volume of tissue.

3. If urine has not been analyzed, submit sample (5–10cc) from bladder, frozen.

4. If serum has not been analyzed, submit sample (10cc), frozen.

5. Send tissue sample to either Dr. Littman or Dr. Wilcock. Send copies of all medical reports (CBC, chem screen, urinalysis, urine protein/creatinine ratio, fecal API and any biopsy results with a copy of pedigree (four generations, if possible) to Dr. Littman or Dr. Wilcock.

Tissue samples may be sent to either Penn or Guelph. SCWTCA will pay for histopathological exams done at Penn or Guelph; owners/breeders are responsible for local vet charges for tissue removal and shipping costs.

PRECAUTIONS TO BE TAKEN WHEN ANESTHETIZING A SOFT COATED WHEATEN TERRIER

PLEASE CALL THE FOLLOWING TO THE ATTENTION OF YOUR VETERINARIAN.

The Soft Coated Wheaten Terrier may react adversely to some anesthetic agents in much the same manner as sighthounds. Barbiturates in particular can cause problems. The following is a protocol recommended by practitioners experienced with the breed.

Pre-op tranquilize with ACE-PROMAZINE/ATROPINE

Induction with VALIUM/KETAMINE

Maintenance with ISOFLUORANE

Although Isofluorane is more expensive than other inhalant anesthetics, because it is so quickly metabolized by the patient, resulting in rapid recovery even in high risk patients, it is fast becoming the anesthetic of choice among most veterinarians.

These recommendations for anesthetizing the Soft Coated Wheaten Terrier were made at the Health Symposium (Montgomery County KC 1993) by George Jeitles, DVM (Health Committee Chair, SCWTCA) and Daniel Burnside, VMD as well as long-time Soft Coated Wheaten Terrier breeders.

Soft Coated Wheaten Terrier Club of America Specialty Winners

YEAR	DOG'S NAME	OWNER(S)	BREEDER(S)
1975	Ch. Raclee's Express West O' Andover CD, ROM	C. Vogels J. Gottlieb	R. Stein
1976	Ch. Butterflow's Dream Weaver	N. & T. Nolan	A. Papaliolios
★	Ch. Raclee's Express West O'Andover CD, ROM	C. Vogels J. Gottlieb	R. Stein
1977	Ch. Briarlyn Dandelion, ROM	L. Penniman	Owner
★	Ch. Briarlyn Dandelion, ROM	L. Penniman	Owner
1978	Ch. Briarlyn Dandelion, ROM	L. Penniman	Owner
★	Ch. Briarlyn Dandelion, ROM	L. Penniman	Owner

YEAR	DOG'S NAME	OWNER(S)	BREEDER(S)
1979	Ch. Kenwoods Armada McDuff	G. & N. Ruehle	E. MacParland & M. Anderson
1980	Ch. Wildflower Woodbalm	J. King & T. Mills	J. Turner
★	Ch. Gleanngay Holliday, ROM	G. Dunlap	Owner
1981	Ch. Gleanngay Motown Moonraker	G. Dunlap & J. Slatin	G. Dunlap
★	Ch. Glenworth Andover Aria	C. Vogels & J. Gottlieb	Mr. & Mrs. E.F. Worth
1982	Ch. Winterwheat's Golden Glo	N.A. Hoffers & D.N. Johnson	B.A. Ekstrom
★	Ch. Claypool's Just Right	L.P. Claypool	Owner
1983	Ch. Marima's Classical Jazz	O.J. & M.L. Lafler	Owners
★	Ch. Azlough Whitecrest Goin West	R.A. & E. Azerolo	P. Godfrey & R. White
1984	Ch. Lontree's Star Waggin	J. Laylon	Owner
★	Ch. Jalin Clanheath 'n' the Clover	G. & B. McNamara	L. Hughes & J. Aray
1985	Ch. Wildflower Stardust, ROM	J. Turner & E. Dalton	Owners
★	Ch. Wildflower Stardust, ROM	J. Turner & E. Dalton	Owners
1986	Ch. Wildflower Stardust, ROM	J. Turner & E. Dalton	Owners
1987	Ch. Andover Song 'n' Dance Man	C. Vogels & J. Gottlieb	Owners
★	Ch. Andover Song 'n' Dance Man	C. Vogels & J. Gottlieb	Owners
1988	Ch. Andover Song 'n' Dance Man	C. Vogels & J. Gottlieb	Owners
★	Ch. Brenmoor's Spark Plug	G. Vlachos & W. Behan	Owners
1989	Ch. Andover Song 'n' Dance Man	C. Vogels & J. Gottlieb	Owners
★	Ch. Andover Song 'n' Dance Man	C. Vogels & J. Gottlieb	Owners
1990	Ch. Bantry Bay Kairo	S.C. Way & R.L. Cotton	S.C. Way & G. Dunlap
★	Ch. Doubloon's Winterwood	E. Landa	Owner
1991	Ch. Doubloon's Master of Illusion	C. Vogels & J. Gottlieb	E. Landa
★	Ch. Doubloon's Master of Illusion	C. Vogels & J. Gottlieb	E. Landa

YEAR	DOG'S NAME	OWNER(S)	BREEDER(S)
1992	Ch. Shar D's Let the Games Begin	S. Boyd & D. Boyd	Owners
★	Ch. Doubloon's Master of Illusion	C. Vogels & J. Gottlieb	E. Landa
1993	Ch. Shar D's Let the Games Begin	S. Boyd & D. Boyd	Owners
1994	Ch. Andover Song 'n' Dance Man	C. Vogels & J. Gottlieb	Owners
★	Ch. Doubloon's Happy Go Latte	E. Landa	Owner
1995	Ch. Legacy Wild West Wildflower	R. Hale & J. Caliri	Owners & E. & J. Dalton
1996	Ch. Andover Make A Wish	J. Gottlieb	Owner
★	Ch. Paisley Midnight Sun	K.M. & M.E. McIndoe	Owners
1997	Ch. Cascade Shaunessey	D. Greenwald	C. Wambach & L. Wolter
1998	Ch. Kaylinn's August Moon	K. Baird-Zwier & D. Zwier	Owners
★	Ch. Kaylinn's August Moon	K. Baird-Zwier & D. Zwier	Owners

★ *Denotes roving specialty*

Bibliography

All Wheaten owners owe it to themselves and their dogs to read and learn about caring for their Wheatens. Following is a list of books that I have found to be useful. Some are out of print, but may be found through an out of print book dealer, a tag sale or a flea market. They are worth the effort of a diligent search. While the list is by no means complete, it should serve as a core collection for the well-read Wheaten enthusiast.

HISTORY

Holmes, Maureen. *The Wheaten Years.* Orland Park, Ill.: Alpha Beta Press, 1977.

———. *The Softcoated Wheaten Terrier.* Ireland: Printed by Racmo, Meppel.

Horner, Tom. *Terriers of the World.* London: Faber and Faber, 1984.

O'Connor, Margaret A. *Soft Coated Wheaten Terriers.* Neptune City, N.J.: T.F.H. Publications, 1990. (Reissue of her 1974 book, *How to Raise and Train a Soft-Coated Wheaten Terrier.*)

Soft Coated Wheaten Terrier Club of America. *Celebrating Ten Years of AKC Registration.* 1986.

———. *The Soft Coated Wheaten Terrier Yearbook.* Privately published, 1990.

Vesley, Roberta A. *The Complete Soft Coated Wheaten Terrier.* New York: Howell Book House, 1991.

Vogels, Cindy, ed. *The Soft Coated Wheaten Terrier Yearbook, 1983-1987*. Boulder, Colo.: Index Publishers, 1988.

—————. *The Soft Coated Wheaten Terrier Yearbook, 1988*. Boulder, Colo.: Index Publishers, 1989.

—————. *The Soft Coated Wheaten Terrier Yearbook, 1989*. Boulder, Colo.: Index Publishers, 1990.

CARE AND BEHAVIOR

American Kennel Club. *The Complete Dog Book for Kids*. New York: Howell Book House, 1996.

Anderson, Moira K. *Coping With Sorrow on the Loss of Your Pet*. Los Angeles: Peregrine Press, 1987.

Animal Medical Center. *The Complete Book of Dog Health*. New York: Macmillan, 1985.

Barish, Eileen. *Vacationing with Your Pet*. Scottsdale, Ariz.: Pet Friendly Publications, 1994.

Burger, I.H. ed. *The Waltham Book of Companion Animal Nutrition*. Tarrytown, N.Y.: Pergamon, 1993.

Campbell, William E. *Owner's Guide to Better Behavior in Dogs and Cats*. Goleta, Calif.: American Veterinary Publications, 1986.

Coffman, Howard D. *The Dry Dog Food Reference*. Nashua, N.H.: Pig Dog Press, 1995.

Collins, Donald R. *The Collins Guide to Dog Nutrition*. New York: Howell Book House, 1987.

Dorosz, Edmund R. BSA, DVM. *Let's Cook For Our Dogs*. Alberta, Canada: Our Pets Inc., 1993.

Gerstenfeld, Sheldon L. *The Dog Care Book*. Reading, Mass.: Addison-Wesley, 1989.

Mindell, Earl, R. Ph, Ph.D and Elizabeth Renaghan. *Earl Mindell's Nutrition and Health Guide for Dogs*. Rocklin, Calif.: Prima Publishing, 1998.

Rutherford, Clarice. *How to Raise a Puppy You Can Live With*. Loveland, Colo.: Alpine Publications, 1981.

Shoemaker, Marjorie C. *Soft Coated Wheaten Terrier, A Complete and Reliable Handbook*. Neptune City, N.J.: TFH Publications.

Soft Coated Wheaten Terrier Club of America. *The Soft Coated Wheaten Terrier Owner's Manual*. 1984.

TRAINING

Behan, Kevin. *Natural Training. The Canine Arts Kennel Program. Teach Your Dog by Using His Natural Instincts*. New York: William Morrow and Company, 1992.

Benjamin, Carol Lea. *Dog Problems: A Professional Trainer's Guide to Preventing and Correcting Aggression, Destructiveness, Housebreaking Problems . . . and Much, Much More*. New York: Howell Book House, 1989.

—————. *Mother Knows Best*. New York: Howell Book House, 1985.

———. *Second-Hand Dog.* New York: Howell Book House, 1988.

Climer, Jerry. *How to Raise a Dog When Nobody's Home.* Jackson, Mich.: Penny Dreadful Publishers, 1983.

Davis, Kathy Diamond. *Therapy Dogs: Training Your Dog to Reach Others.* New York: Howell Book House, 1992.

Evans, Job Michael. *The Evans Guide for Civilized City Canines.* New York: Howell Book House, 1988.

———. *The Evans Guide for Housetraining Your Dog.* New York: Howell Book House, 1987.

Fox, Michael W. *Superdog: Raising the Perfect Canine Companion.* New York: Howell Book House, 1990.

Haggerty, Capt. Arthur and Carol Lee Benjamin. *Dog Tricks. Teaching Your Dog to Be Useful, Fun and Entertaining.* New York: Howell Book House, 1988.

Ross, John and Barbara McKinney. *Dog Talk. Training Your Dog Through a Canine Point of View.* New York: St. Martin's Press, 1992.

Wolters, Richard A. *Home Dog.* New York: E.P. Dutton, 1984.

SHOWING

Alston, George G., with Connie Vanacore. *The Winning Edge—Show Ring Secrets.* New York: Howell Book House, 1992.

Craige, Patricia. *Born to Win—Breed to Succeed.* Wilsonville, Ore: Doral Publishing, 1997.

Forsyth, Jane and Robert Forsyth. *The Forsyth Guide to Successful Dog Showing.* New York: Howell Book House, 1975.

Hall, Lynn. *Dog Showing for Beginners.* New York: Howell Book House, 1994.

Sabella, Frank T. *The Art of Handling Show Dogs.* Hollywood, Calif.: B&E Publications, 1980.

Vanacore, Connie. *Dog Showing—An Owner's Guide.* New York: Howell Book House, 1990.

BREEDING

Lee, Muriel P. *The Whelping and Rearing of Puppies.* Neptune N.J.: TFH Publications.

Seranne, Ann. *The Joy of Breeding Your Own Show Dog.* New York: Howell Book House, 1980.

Walkowicz, Chris and Bonnie Wicox, D.V.M. *Successful Dog Breeding—The Complete Handbook of Canine Midwifery, 2nd Ed.* New York: Howell Book House, 1994.

Willis, Malcolm B. *Genetics of the Dog.* London: H.F. & G. Witherby, Ltd., 1989.

GENERAL

Buland, Susan. *Canine Source Book.* Wilsonville, Ore.: Doral Publishing, 1990.

Gilbert, Edward, Jr. and Thelma Brown. *K-9 Structure and Terminology.* New York: Howell Book House, 1995.

Lane, Marion S. *The Humane Society of the United States, Complete Guide to Dog Care.* New York: Little Brown, 1998.

Pavia, Audrey and Betsy Siikora Siino. *Dogs on the Web.* New York: MIS Press, 1997.

School of Veterinary Medicine, U.C. Davis, Mordecai Siegal, ed. *U.C. Davis School of Veterinary Medicine Book of Dogs.* New York: Harper Collins, 1995.

Index

The Author

R oberta Vesley, a native of Long Island (New York), has been a breeder and exhibitor of Soft Coated Wheaten Terriers since 1969, prior to the breed's official AKC recognition in 1973. She is the author of *The Complete Soft Coated Wheaten Terrier* (New York: Howell Book House, 1991).

She joined the staff of The American Kennel Club in 1975 and served as its library director from 1980 until 1991. She was a founding member and past President of the Soft Coated Wheaten Terrier Club of Metropolitan New York, a Director of The Soft Coated Wheaten Terrier Club of America and a Director and Secretary of Long Island Kennel Club. She has been a guest curator for The Dog Museum and has written on dogs for *World Book, Readers Digest* and the *AKC Gazette*.